After He's Gone

A Guide for Widowed and Divorced Women

Barbara Tom Jowell
and
Donnette Schwisow

A BIRCH LANE PRESS BOOK
Published by Carol Publishing Group

A Birch Lane Press Book
Published by Carol Publishing Group
Birch Lane Press is a registered trademark of Carol Communications, Inc.

Editorial, sales and distribution, rights and permissions inquiries should be
addressed to Carol Publishing Group, 120 Enterprise Avenue, Secaucus, N.J.
07094.

In Canada: Canadian Manda Group, One Atlantic Avenue, Suite 105, Toronto,
Ontario, M6K 3E7

Carol Publishing Group books may be purchased in bulk at special discounts for
sales promotion, fund-raising, or educational purposes. Special editions can be
created to specifications. For details, contact Special Sales Department, Carol
Publishing Group, 120 Enterprise Avenue, Secaucus, N.J. 07094.

Manufactured in the United States of America
10 9 8 7 6 5 4 3 2 1

Library of Congress Cataloging-in-Publication Data

Schwisow, Donnette.
    After he's gone : a guide for widowed and divorced women /
Donnette Schwisow and Barbara Tom Jowell.
        p. cm.
    "A Birch Lane Press book".
    Includes bibliographical references (p.) and index.
    ISBN 1–55972–433–1 (hard)
    1. Widows—United States—Life skills guides. 2. Divorce—United
States—Handbooks, manuals, etc. I. Jowell, Barbara Tom.
II. Title.
HQ1058.5.U5S39   1997
646.7'0086'54—dc21   97–41073
                                                          CIP

To Our Lunch Bunch

CONTENTS

Preface   ix
Acknowledgments   xiv

PART I: WHERE YOU ARE NOW

1   Feeling Better Right This Minute   3
2   Divorced   12
3   Widowed   40

PART II: PRACTICAL MATTERS

4   Creating Your Own Support Group   63
5   Teaching Others How to Treat You   76
6   Your Personal Bank Account of Life Experiences   85
7   Setting and Accomplishing Your Goals   100
8   Landing a Job or Starting a Business   108
9   The Professionals You Work With   123
10   Protecting Your Assets   137
11   Buying or Selling a Home   162
12   New Car Fever   178

PART III: FROM DOWN THERE TO UP HERE

13   Traveling   189
14   Socializing and Dating Again   199
15   Onward and Upward   211

Bibliography   223
Index   227

Preface

In 1988, we became two among the 50 percent of women married before 1974 who had experienced divorce or widowhood.

DONNETTE: *I was happily married to a good-looking forty-nine-year-old attorney whose recent bypass surgery had just been deemed highly successful. He was back to jogging five to six miles a day. We were enjoying our lake cabin and spent happy hours sailing our sailboat on the weekends.*

Due to a long meeting one Thursday afternoon, I was late getting home. I swung my car into the garage, noting with some disgust that Mac's car wasn't there. He hadn't arrived home either, and we had to be dressed and at a dinner party in less than thirty minutes. As I hurriedly gathered my purse and briefcase, I saw the reflection of our neighbor, Wayne, in the car's rearview mirror. He approached me as I got out of the car. "Donnette," said Wayne, "I have some very sad news. Mac had another heart attack, and he didn't make it this time."

BARBARA: *I was leaving the house to give a speech at the Boys Club when the phone rang. In a still, calm voice, a friend told me that my husband of twenty-seven years was having affairs. Not singular, but plural. Affairs. I hung up the phone, my mind churning. We had had many disagreements over the years, but not this. Not this. I swung my purse to my shoulder, locked the front door, and drove to the Boys' Club.*

How did I give the speech? How did I keep from throwing

myself onto the tattered couch in that little cement-block building and sobbing? Shock. Like a person after a car wreck, I walked around, breathed, and spoke. But my mind was locked in shock. I gave the speech I'd been planning and no one suspected that my life would never be the same."

We had been dear friends for twelve years. We were members of the same closely knit "lunch bunch" of seven women and had worked side by side as volunteers in the community. We never dreamed we'd be facing the biggest transition of our lives at the same time.

In the early months following our becoming single again, there were answers we needed, and we wanted those answers in a hurry. When we first found ourselves in the midst of dealing with the concerns of life after he was gone, we had neither the time nor emotional strength to wade through pounds of prose to find the answers to our questions. We yearned for concise, to-the-point information that would give us step-by-step practical survival techniques. We searched for a single book that would empathize, instruct, and encourage. Instead, we found ourselves poring through miles of long paragraphs.

We envisioned a book format that would feature a chapter for each of our major concerns. We could enjoy a few true-life stories because tales of success are inspiring; primarily, however, we wanted just the facts, ma'am, just the facts."

We were unable to find either the inspirational boost or the concise educational material we needed in less than twelve to fourteen publications. So we spent months with our heads buried in various books and in consultation with lawyers, accountants, and insurance professionals. Then we'd be on the phone to each other, sharing our information about new health insurance, selling the house, or buying a car.

As we began to share our accumulated knowledge with others, a friend suggested that we put together a program for other suddenly single women. Both of us had had considerable professional public-speaking experience, so our friend's idea began to germinate! In October 1989, we held our first "Women in Transition" workshop.

Now, after eight years of presenting seminars and workshops, we have written *After He's Gone,* a result of our personal and workshop experiences. We also educated ourselves as to professional studies concerning the needs of hundreds of thousands of other women who had found themselves single again.

A variety of studies and surveys revealed sobering statistics. Mentioned above from a study conducted by the National Center for Health Statistics was the fact that, of the women married before 1974, 50 percent have experienced divorce or widowhood, and this figure is rapidly growing with the maturation of the Baby Boomers. Another survey cited that two-thirds of all women with children will spend at least part of their lifetimes as single mothers. A depressing statistic proven all too often in our workshops is from *Divorce and Annulments,* a report by the U.S. Bureau of the Census: "The average marriage in the United States lasts only seven years."

The U.S. Bureau of the Census, Business and Professional Women's Foundation released statistics showing that 73 percent of women die single, 80 percent to 90 percent of all women will be responsible for their own finances at some point, and 80 percent of widows now living in poverty were not poor before the death of their husbands. A three-year study by Jan L. Warner and Jan Collins Stucker, authors of a column for those who have divorced, separated, or survived the death of a spouse, showed that only 21 percent of the women respondents knew the family's financial status before divorce, 95 percent of those who responded felt unprepared to deal with the economics of divorce, and 81 percent of women interviewed were concerned about educating themselves to enter or reenter the workplace.

If you are feeling emotionally exhausted or frightened by the economics of being alone again, or if you are overwhelmed with the prospect of educating yourself to enter the workplace, take heart! The good news is that you *can* do it! You *can* become self-sufficient and self-confident. You *can* find your dream lifework or career. No, you are *not* too old, or too young, or too uneducated. You can study and you can learn! Christopher Hayes, Ph.D., research director of the National Center for Women and Retirement Research at Long Island University in New York, reports from a nationwide survey of recently divorced women that more than half felt free to be themselves for the first time. For these women, the divorce experience "became a growth-enhancing transition that led to a stronger sense of self, to greater satisfaction with life." An estate attorney, who works with widows says, "It is so gratifying to watch women grow, gain confidence in themselves, and actually blossom in their new roles."

You can become one of these women who have triumphed over transition. We designed this book to help you become one of the winners. The book is divided into three parts: Part I: "Where You Are Now," Part II: "Practical Matters," and Part III: "From Down There to Up Here." Chapter 1, "Feeling Better Right This Minute," is a short, empathetic yet pragmatic chapter which focuses on things you can do right this minute to feel better. "Divorced" and "Widowed" are detailed chapters dealing with your particular situation.

Part II: "Practical Matters" helps you reenter the world outside death or divorce. The chapters "Creating Your Own Support Group" and "Teaching Others How to Treat You" affirm our need for others as well as our need to be treated with respect by others. "Your Personal Bank Account of Life Experiences" will build your self-confidence as you learn to identify the skills, experience, and education you have amassed just by living life, not only from your formal education. You will set and achieve goals for your new life in the chapter "Setting and Accomplishing Your Goals."

Whether you're in the market for on-the-job training, a job to help finance completing your education, a better-paying job because of new budget constraints, or the dream position of your career, the first portion of "Landing a Job or Starting a Business" will give you the specific techniques you need. The hopeful entrepreneur will find her tips in the second portion of the chapter.

The next chapters will give you confidence in the world of business, finance, and self-care. Tips on finding just the right lawyer, accountant, insurance agent, or financial planner are offered in "The Professionals You Work With." The chapter "Protecting Your Assets" deals with money—from opening checking accounts to establishing credit, making investments, choosing insurance—life, health, long-term care, homeowner's, and automobile—and designing your ultimate asset protection—your will. Useful information about buying and selling houses and cars as well as dollar-saving travel tips are included in the chapters "Buying or Selling a Home" and "New Car Fever."

You are brought back to the personal in Part III with "Traveling" and "Socializing and Dating Again" where there are some tips for becoming acquainted with new friends and reacquainted with old friends. If dating again leads you to finding Mr. Right, there is important advice on learning about the financial aspect of each other's lives. The book concludes with an "Onward and Upward" chapter, which includes a short review of some of the key points covered in *After He's Gone*, a list of the most frequently asked questions (and answers) from our workshops, and suggestions from our seminars.

You are going through a very difficult transition in your life. Please know that you can and *will* proceed upward from where you are now. You *will* get from down there to up here. *You can do it. The time to begin is now.*

Acknowledgments

Our heartfelt thanks to the following people:

For Their Professional Expertise

Roberta Aldridge, Langston Realtors, Midland, Texas

John H. Alpers, CFP, managing director, Gateway Financial Strategies, LLC, Boulder, Colorado, a registered investment adviser (RIA)

Linda Bond, for her priceless savvy about agents, query letters, proposals, and how to get started writing a book!

Carrie Cantor, our wonderful editor, who thought of things that never entered our minds!

Robert H. Dawson, Board-Certified Estate Planning and Probate Law, Texas Board of Legal Specialization, Cotton, Bledsoe, Tighe and Dawson, Attorneys-at-Law, Midland, Texas

Marvin H. Feldman, ChFC, CLU, The Feldman Agency, East Liverpool, Ohio

W. Clay Gaston, Board-Certified Civil Trial Law, Texas Board of Legal Specialization, Canon, Short and Gaston, Attorneys-at-Law, Midland, Texas

Ann Harper, for excellent critiques of our seminars and advice on book proposals

Jim Hill, Insurance Agent, Jim Hill Insurance, Midland, Texas

Robert Kaufman, CFS, CPA, Midland, Texas

Kathy Montgomery, Consumer Banker, NationsBank, Midland, Texas

Mark Mercer, M.S., LPC, Social Work Director, Hospice of Midland, Inc.

Peter Rubie, our great agent, who never lost faith in us
Suzanne Smith, HNB Mortgage, Midland, Texas
Betty Sumner, for her excellent word-processing skills!
Carole Symnonette, Regional Manager, Texas Association of
    Business and Chambers of Commerce
N. Mott Williamson, CPA, Shareholder: Wurster, Armstrong and
    Williamson, PC, Midland, Texas
P. T. Wurster, CPA, Shareholder: Wurster, Armstrong and
    Williamson, PC, Midland, Texas

A Special Word of Gratitude To

Our Lunch Bunch: Suzy Boldrick, Sara Fry, Louan Rogers,
    Betty Sumner, and Mary Jane Young, for your love, support,
    cheerleading and proofreading!
Shelley, Chip, Tricia, and Joe (Barbara's daughters and their
    husbands) and Ron (Donnette's husband), for your love, pride,
    and faith in us, to say nothing of the countless problems
    solved, favors graciously granted, and errands cheerfully run
    on our behalf!
The Junior League, for years of believing in us, encouraging us,
    and giving us the opportunity to develop a wide range of
    skills: administrative, development, organizational, public
    speaking and writing, to name a few! A Fortune 500 corpora-
    tion could not have offered better training, and we are forever
    grateful.

PART I

WHERE YOU ARE NOW

Feeling Better Right This Minute

SUDDENLY ALONE: FEELINGS AND FEARS

When Joy Kester was widowed, she felt safe at home—until the dark night when the alarm of her security system screamed out a warning. Waking up in a panic, she realized she had never planned what to do if her alarm went off.

"I thought it was enough that I had an alarm system," Joy said. "I had not thought about whom to call or what to do when it did go off."

When you are suddenly alone, many things happen to you. You wake up at night terrified. Some mornings you want to pull the covers over your head and never get up. You want to talk to someone, anyone—and when you're with people you can't think of anything to say. You cry over commercials for long-distance telephone services, and get furious when the car in front of you sits too long at the light. It seems as if all at the same time your washing machine breaks, the registration expires on the car, and the toilet overflows. You feel as if no one understands, and sometimes you wonder if anyone really cares.

Please accept these words of reassurance: You are not silly or a big baby or crazy. You are alone, and that isn't what you had expected at this point in your life. That can make you angry, afraid, sad, and disoriented. Someday this stage will pass, but right now you just want to figure out how to cope.

You may cry. That's all right. You might not need to cry. People may marvel at how well you cope, or they may seem bothered by your ability to function in the midst of a terrible situation. And that's all right too. Your body and your mind are struggling the best they can with an overload of shock and pain.

Through our own loss and our work with many women who have experienced the anxiety of divorce or widowhood, we have found some tips to help you deal with the darkness, face the day and get control of your life.

SURVIVAL TIP

You will feel better right now—whether it's morning, noon, or night—if you make a list of your fears and concerns. Whatever is bothering you, write it down. Once your concerns are down on paper, it's easier to systematically develop solutions. Ask for a friend's viewpoint if your thinking gets muddled.

AT NIGHT

For many women, the hardest time is at night. The darkness seems to enlarge fears just like a magnifying glass. The house makes the same sounds it does during the day, but at night those sounds are terrifying. The same money worries are there during the day, but somehow the darkness is a catalyst to ignite all this magnification.

How can you shed a little light on your own personal darkness?

Realize that things will be worse at night. It's not you, it's just the way it is. Donnette's Southern Baptist grandmother used to say that night is the Devil's playtime. The negative just seems to lie in wait for darkness to come.

Imagine yourself in a safe, tranquil situation.

DONNETTE: *To counter the darkness after I was widowed, I used to envision laying my head in the lap of an angel, who comforted and surrounded me with good feelings. I would imagine every detail, from the way the ground looked to the feathery touch of the angel's wings. I could hear the river trickling by and see the white clouds. I was calmed and comforted and finally I would go to sleep.*

Make your home feel safe and secure.

- Call your local police station for a security check. They may advise keyed dead-bolt locks, new solid-core doors, and window guards. Perhaps they will suggest a new alarm system.
- If the police cannot come to your home, call a reputable locksmith and an alarm system company for their recommendations. Shop around and get the best prices possible, but do not compromise on quality.
- Perhaps you can save money by installing exterior motion sensor lights yourself. Is there a handyman in your office who could install keyed double-deadbolt locks and window guards for you?

If you feel unsafe in your home, begin to make your home secure now, today, this minute!

Make a plan. Joy Kester had a nice new alarm system, but she had no idea what to do if it went off. So after her "alarming" night, she sat down and planned what to do if her burglar alarm rang. She programmed her telephone to automatically dial 911 when she pushes a button, and she has mentally mapped an escape route if she needs one.

Find the calm of the night. Nighttime doesn't have to be a horror story. Find things that will calm you in the night and reach for them when you are afraid or restless.

- Put a stack of your favorite books on your bedside table (unless your favorites are Stephen King stories).
- Make sure you can easily reach a light.
- Keep a cassette tape or CD of mellow, calming music ready to play.

- Set your radio dial for music, rather than an all-night news station that might be broadcasting bad news.

Don't rely on alcohol or drugs for sleep. You will sleep, eventually—your body will demand it. Let it happen naturally.

Write down your thoughts. If you find that you can't sleep because you're worrying about all the things you have to do, don't lie there in the dark agonizing about them. Sit up, turn on the light, and make lists. List all the things you have to do, all the things that worry you, questions you need to remember to ask, papers you have to find. Tomorrow you can check off items as you accomplish them.

If your feelings are running rampant, write them down. Try keeping a journal. You can record anything you feel, anything you want to remember—or even things you'd rather forget. Draw little sketches in the margins if you feel like it, make up poems, compose songs. You can write anything you want—it's your bed, your room, your journal.

Get comfortable.

- Just because your bedroom has always been arranged the way it is, doesn't mean it has to continue to be that way. Take over both closets if you want, rearrange your dresser drawers, or shove your bed against the wall.
- Make a stack of magazines, or throw out all the magazines that are cluttering your room.
- Pile up all the pillows, pick out soft sheets, put your down comforter on top.
- Wear your most comfortable sleepwear, even if it's ugly. Sleep in socks, or even your slippers, if your feet are cold.
- Put a glass of water on your bedside table so you can drink it in the middle of the night if you happen to get thirsty.

Cut the consumption of stimulants. If you're unable to sleep or you're waking up in a panic in the middle of the night, think about what you've had to drink or eat during the day. How has your intake changed since you've been alone? Have you been downing coffee after coffee or sipping caffeinated soft drinks? Are you eating those comforting chocolates by the truckload?

Some women find their sleep habits are disrupted by one cup of coffee, even if they've had it earlier in the day. Alcohol, though it may make you drowsy at first, can often awaken you in the middle of the night. Substitute the things which cause your wakefulness with soporifics such as herbal teas (not ginseng!) or milk.

Don't choose the wrong movies and TV programs to watch. Avoid like the plague shows in which a woman alone in a house is tortured by aliens, monsters, ghosts, appliance salesmen, Freddy Krueger, an ex-husband.

Call a friend. Do you have a friend or acquaintance in a similar situation—going through a divorce or recently widowed? Make a pact to call each other, any time of the day or night, to discuss your concerns. Your friend may have just found a solution to the very problem you're dealing with now! We found such comfort in being able to pick up the phone and call each other any time of the day or night.

Don't feel as though you have to sleep just because it's night. Who makes those rules, anyhow?

IN THE MORNING

For Barbara, the toughest time during her divorce was the morning.

BARBARA: *Some mornings upon wakening, I would have a dreadful sense of foreboding. I would feel just like a child who has been in trouble with her parents the day before. I didn't want to face the day because I thought it, too, would be full of trouble. At first when I'd wake up and for about two seconds, I'd feel all right, then the shock would hit. Sometimes it would take me a while to remember what the matter was. Then I'd put my head under the covers. When the shock and anxiety was worst for me, I did this: each morning before I opened my eyes, I said, "Okay, Barb, think of one positive, exciting thing you're going to do today—just one thing." Once I had directed my thoughts in a positive direction, I would have far less trouble facing the day.*

Here are some tips on how to face the day:

Plan some lying-in-bed time. Set your alarm for earlier than you actually need to get up so you can pull the covers back over your head for a while—resetting the alarm for later, of course.

Get an alarm clock that awakens you gently. Set the clock radio to a station you really like. If you have ever had an alarm-driven coffeepot, drag it out of its box and put it to use. Nothing will get you out of bed better than the smell of coffee brewing. Use decaffeinated coffee if possible.

Make a plan before you go to bed at night. Lay out the clothes you'll wear. Write down the things you need to do the next day. Go to bed knowing at least one thing you're going to do when you wake up.

Keep an appointment calendar beside your bed. Before you even get out of bed, look to see what appointments you have, with addresses and items you need to bring. If you have no appointments scheduled, write down the things you'd like to do. Plan your visits to the library, trips to the supermarket, a time to clean out your closet. The more in control you feel, the easier it will be to get up and face the day.

Have some food in your kitchen that's worth eating. Get the kinds of cereals *you* like, be sure that there's milk, or bread for toasting, some kind of fruit. Make it worth your while to get up in the morning.

Fix your hair and put on your makeup when you get up. Don't wait till late in the day to take care of yourself.

Follow the advice of positive thinkers, such as Zig Ziglar. One of the top salespeople in the world, Ziglar suggests that you sit up, swing your legs over the side of the bed, clap your hands and say, "This is going to be a *great* day."

DURING THE DAY

Here are some tips on how to counter the negative thoughts and feelings you have when you feel alone:

Find comfort in your spiritual beliefs. Consult a higher power. Pray; go to your church, synagogue, or temple.

Keep busy, even when you're experiencing the first numbing effects of shock. Maintain that list of things you have to do. Put a check mark by each item as you do it. One of the effects of shock may be that you forget what you're doing or need to do.

Don't underestimate yourself. You have surprising resources inside you. You will come through this.

If you're lying down, sit up. If you're sitting, stand. If you're standing, walk around.

Call someone. Say this: "How are you?" Force yourself to listen to the answer. If you have to, pretend you're interested. Do this *before* you say a word about yourself.

Change clothes. Put on something bright and clean. Don't even think about putting on uncomfortable shoes.

Eat properly.

- Stop eating whatever junk is around the house.
- Order in, buy something at the grocery store that's easy to prepare, or go to the cafeteria to get those vegetables that seem to be too much trouble to fix.
- Try eating low-fat microwave popcorn instead of french fries.
- If you have lost your appetite altogether, don't worry. Your appetite *will* return. Those friends who are insisting, "But you must eat *something*," are concerned about you. Just explain to them that nausea, diarrhea, and loss of appetite are all normal symptoms of shock. If your symptoms persist, consult your physician.

Take your friends up on their offers to help. It's your job to let your friends know how they can help you. Why not call one of them when you need a ride to the airport or a prescription picked up at the drugstore? Remember that friends and family really want to help you. They just don't know how. They mean it when they say, "Please let me know if I can do anything, anything at all."

Find a new friend or rediscover a lost one. (See chapter 4, "Creating Your Own Support Group.") Studies have shown that lonely people have weakened immune systems. Remember what your mother used to say: "To have a friend, be one." Maybe someone needs your help even more than you need theirs.

Break out of your routine. Take a different route, go to a new place, find a new bookstore, take a peek in a local museum. Try to do something different *every day*, even if it's something small.

Begin a new career or master a new skill. Do something you've always wanted to do. You have the freedom to do this, you know. (See chapter 6, "Your Personal Bank Account of Life's Experiences.")

Don't be so hard on yourself. The confusion, depression, anger, and sadness is part of your loss. Do not blame yourself for these feelings. (See chapter 2, "Stages of Grief from the About-to-Be-Divorced Woman's Point of View," or chapter 3, "Stages of Grief From the Widow's Point of View.")

Turn up the music. You can make major attitude adjustments through music. Turn on the radio, pop in a cassette tape or CD, and dance around the kitchen. Whistle. Sing out loud. This is your place, and you can do anything you want. Avoid heart-wrenching country-western songs, unless you feel like wallowing in sorrow.

Set aside ten to twenty minutes every day and practice calming yourself. Close your eyes, breathe deeply. Tell yourself, "I have all the resources I need to care for myself. I can do it." Breathe slowly and repeat that phrase to yourself with each exhalation. Concentrate on the breath as it comes in and the breath as it goes out. Relax from head to toe.

Start exercising. Go to the nearest health club, walk the mall, ride a stationary bike, wander through your neighborhood with a friend. You'll feel better, and you'll probably find it improves how you look, too.

Look at problems as opportunities. Cancel the negative thoughts as they come and try to be open to the smallest opportunity for joy. Sometimes you have to actively work at seeing the good behind the hassles you're going through, but you'll find that trying makes a tremendous difference.

Don't rush into things. Give yourself plenty of time—at least a year—before making major decisions.

Seek help. If your feelings are too much to cope with alone, contact others. A list of organizations that help members cope with everything from depression to headaches appears in almost every local newspaper. Your county health organization has a list of professionals trained to deal with emotional needs. Read chapter 4, "Creating Your Own Support Group."

Give yourself permission to be happy, when happiness starts coming back to you. And it will. It will.

2

Divorced

MAKING THE DECISION

Regardless of whether a divorce is your decision or your spouse's, it can be one of the most agonizing times in a person's life.

When you make the decision to get a divorce, be *very sure* that you are *totally* committed, because you are about to embark on the most stressful period of your life. If your decision is made and you are positive you will never think, "Oh my gosh, why did I ever start this?" then forge ahead. There will be times when you will struggle through quicksand and feel it will never end. But at some point you will finally be on the other side of the divorce, and will feel as Barbara did—as if the sun had come up...shining brightly. Every time she hears someone is getting a divorce, she thinks, "How thankful I am to be where I am, completely through the journey and happily on my way!"

When It's Your Decision

If the divorce is your choice, plan ahead. Give yourself time to get your "ducks in a row." No matter how cold and calculating this sounds, it is a must. Even when you think you have thought through everything, you probably have not. Mentally, men treat a divorce like a business. Therefore, you must also think in a businesslike manner even though it may be difficult. Generally women come out with the short end of the stick. You must learn and learn fast, especially if you have not been involved in the financial side of your marriage.

When It's Not Your Decision

If your husband surprises you and asks for a divorce, stall for time. You must work quickly to find out all you can about the family finances. If he files for divorce, you must delay before making the divorce final in order to gather all the information possible to make a better settlement for yourself. Four things *not* to waste your time doing when your husband asks for a divorce:

1. If the marriage is over, this is not the time to do as Amy did. She wanted to win back her husband's affections, so she took off for a health spa. By the time she emerged six weeks later, twelve pounds slimmer and gorgeous, her husband had hidden the assets so thoroughly she never retrieved a major portion of that which was due her.
2. Do not tear yourself to pieces trying to figure out what you did wrong.
3. Do not destroy his BMW with a pickax. Better it should be included in the division of community property.
4. Do not sell yourself short. You are a lot more capable than you may give yourself credit for. You *can* do this.

Who Goes and Who Stays

Once the decision to divorce has been made, you need to separate—either to different houses or at least different parts of your own house. If you are unwilling to leave your home and your husband cannot be persuaded to leave the residence peacefully, you will probably have to hire a lawyer to handle the separation. The lawyer will obtain a court order that sets forth your rights and your husband's rights during the divorce period. This court order is called a restraining order, an injunction, or a similar term. The order will define not only the right to the use of the home, but also possession and visitation with children, and use of funds of your joint estate. It also authorizes a court to punish either spouse for failure to comply with the order.

STAGES OF GRIEF

As you contemplate a divorce, go through a divorce, and recover from a divorce, you will experience the same emotions as a person experiencing the death of a loved one. You are during this time experiencing the death of life as you have known it. You will feel the pain that comes with that loss.

This pain, in all its forms, is grief. It may muddle your thinking, destroy your sleep, rip through you like a knife when you least expect it. Grief has many stages of healing. It will take time, and you are impatient. You wonder why you feel so out of control, so lost, so miserable, even angry, and more than anything, you want to know the answer to the question, "When will I recover?"

Today, right this minute, give yourself permission to be patient with your pain. You cannot rush it, you cannot jump past it. Just take a deep breath and say out loud, "I give myself permission to be patient with this pain."

We have done seminars all across the United States to help people deal with their loss, and there is one question we are always asked. Men and women want to know, "When will this end?" Behind that question is another. That hidden question is, "Will this pain *ever* end?"

The answer, simply, is yes. Yes, but...we cannot tell you when. What we can tell you is that we have heard from hundreds of people who felt the pain you feel and made it through. We can give you some things to do that will make you feel better. We can help you understand your grief.

Shock

If the divorce is not your decision, the first reaction you may feel is shock. You may have known, suspected, dreaded, or worried that something was going to happen, but the moment it does, you are shocked. Your shock may last a few seconds, like a slap in the face. On the other hand, there may be weeks when you say, "I just cannot *believe* it."

Our bodies and minds are intricate. Shock can help you through the first moments or days when the divorce is a certainty. It is a padding of disbelief that cushions your loss.

Susan, a participant in one of our seminars in South Carolina, said that after she found that her husband had been unfaithful and she realized divorce was inevitable, she felt that her brain was locked in shock. She felt immobilized. She found herself sitting and staring, unable to work or take action. She was absolutely and totally overwhelmed by the enormity of what she knew she had to do. She felt as if she had been hit in the head with a brick.

If you feel this way:

- Make a list of things you have to do. One of the effects of shock may be that you forget what you are doing or need to do.
- Let your friends help you when they offer. You may feel as if you are imposing, but they would not have offered had they not wanted to be a support.
- Do not try to look at the entire "big picture." Break it down into small, manageable pieces so it will not be so overwhelming.

Know this: Shock does not last. Your grief has some more stages yet to work through.

Anger

You are angry? Well, we don't blame you. You did not expect your marriage to end like this. You have suffered a terrible injustice. You would not be human if you did not try to find someone or something to blame.

Do this right now:

Make a list of all the things that make you mad. Do not forget to throw in things like not knowing how to program the VCR or work the answering machine. Absolutely nothing is too petty for this list. Write down even those things you know you should be grateful for but you find aggravating...like your mother who calls too often. Who would have ever suspected that nice as you are, you would be angry about so many things?

Look at the list. Are there things that cannot be changed? Mark them off. Are there items listed that you know will change on their own? Put a check mark by them. What's left? How about the things that make you mad that you can do something about? Circle them.

Make another list—just of the circled items. How can you change them? One by one, little by little, work on this list. If you are infuriated by all the unfinished business left by your loss, work on it bit by bit, every day.

Do the people who are trying to help you make you furious? It is your job to let them know how they can help you without making you angry. Are they treating you like a child? Give them an alternative. Try saying something like, "Thanks for the offer to handle my money, but that is something I am going to have to do myself. However, I would love to have you suggest some of your favorite mutual funds."

You may be angry at yourself for things you did or did not do while you were married. You could have, should have, would have done things differently, if it had been possible. Carolyn had devoted all of her time to her children. She always put their needs and wishes before the needs of her husband. She thought he should feel the same way she did about the children. When her husband wanted her attention, she always answered, "In a minute..." He had a secretary who was very willing to give him all the attention he wanted. Carolyn had to learn to forgive herself. You must forgive yourself, too, for all the things you could have, should have, would have done differently. You are human. You make mistakes. The next time you start to think about your own failing, stop. *Make* yourself think of something else, something you *can* do.

You may be angriest at your husband for changing your life so completely by leaving. Your loss is unfair. Anger is normal. It is frustrating to have your plans and expectations for the rest of your life wrecked. If it makes you feel better, spend one evening alone stomping, yelling, throwing inexpensive breakables at the walls. Say out loud all the things that make you angry. Wallow in your anger. Have a pity party.

Then put anger and pity aside. Get back to the business of your life. Being angry and bitter does not hurt the one at whom you are angry...he could care less. Bitterness hurts you. Give it up!

Depression

Depression is normal. It is a part of grief, even if the divorce is your idea. It is not something to be ashamed of. And here is the best thing about depression: *It will pass.*

This is the time to realize that the divorce is actually happening and things are never going to be the way they used to be again. But think about the past. Do you really want things to be the same as before? Make yourself think honestly about the past. Were you truly happy?

Do this right now:

- Make a list of everything that made you happy in and about your marriage. Did these things really make you happy or did they make you feel secure? Mark off just the things that made you feel secure.
- Make a second list and list all the things that made you unhappy about your marriage.
- Compare the lists and be honest with yourself. Is your second list longer than your first?

If there is anything our work in seminars for women in transition has shown, it is that when you are depressed you have trouble believing that simple phrase: *It will pass.* So I will say it again. *It will pass.* Someday this dark cloud will lift and you will see the sun again. You will smile and you will be so surprised that you will not know whether it is all right for you to smile or not.

If you are reading this through a deep depression, we wish we could take your hand and lead you to the brightness up ahead. The majority of the women we have helped through our seminars have told us that after successfully surviving a divorce, they realized that they could handle anything and stand on their own. They became self-confident and had a better self-image because they did something about a bad situation. They enjoyed their privacy. They were free to make their own decisions about their lives without considering someone else. Many times their lives had been put on hold during their marriage. Now they were free to develop their own hopes and dreams.

This is a challenging time for you. But perhaps it can be a time to discover the things that have been hidden inside you.

Right now, try to envision your depression as a long, dark hallway. You are walking through it, slowly. Yes, it seems unending. But look! Down at the other end, there is a door. On the other side of the door, there is light and joy and life. You may not reach that door today, and maybe not tomorrow. But you will reach it. You will open it. You will leave this awful dark corridor of depression behind.

Your depression is a part of grief, and it's normal. But it is not a life sentence.

Acceptance

Then there is acceptance. It comes gradually, mixed in with the everyday grieving. It is the moment you hear a car drive into the driveway and know it is not his car. It never again will be. Acceptance may not come today or tomorrow, but it will come.

BARBARA: *Some of you may suffer this grief as I did.* I grieved while my marriage was still intact. *After my divorce was final, all I felt was complete relief. When Donnette and I started our seminars, I found myself wondering about my grief process. What had happened to it? Would I someday, a few years down the road, sink into a quagmire of grief? After all, this person I had been married to for twenty-seven years had not only been my husband, but he had been in my life from the time I was seven years old. We had grown up together. Was there something wrong with me?*

A good friend finally explained it to me so that it was perfectly logical. I had suffered all the stages of grief, but they had all come before the divorce.

I spent the early part of my marriage in denial and then as the years passed denial was combined with shock. Every time I discovered that my husband was not the person I had always believed him to be, I was shocked. After the shock and denial, there came a period where nothing he did shocked me anymore but I was angry for years. In order to cope with the anger, I filled my days and nights with my children and volunteer work. I replaced him in my life with pleasant activities. Therefore I was able to combine this with more denial and lived what appeared to be a normal, picture-perfect life. I never recognized depression as depression, I called it anxiety. I went through years with a "fear of the unknown." The thing that I wished for the most was what I called inner peace. Now I realize that all of this was a mourning process. It was a dying marriage. After my divorce was final came acceptance, which I call relief and inner peace.

FINDING AN ATTORNEY

Good lawyers provide care, skill, and judgment. Find one who delivers these attributes to and for you.

Shopping Around

- Choose your divorce lawyer more carefully than anything you have ever chosen.
- The least expensive attorney is not necessarily a good buy. This may be the one time not to think about cost because this may be a case of "You get what you pay for."
- The person who needs the best attorney is the woman who has been a wife and a mother—and has not worked outside the home.
- If you have no money, your attorney may be able to obtain a court order mandating that your husband pay for these services.

- Think twice about choosing a friend as your attorney. If you become dissatisfied with the way he or she is handling your case, you will be uncomfortable.

When Janet filed for divorce in Connecticut, she used an old friend as her attorney. She thought he would have her best interest at heart. The divorce did not move along as quickly as Janet wanted. Her lawyer did not thoroughly read the financial material she brought him. She tried to tell him about money she knew her husband had in South America. He had "moonlighted" as a consultant during the thirteen years that they had lived there, working for a major oil company. His consultant partner was holding the money for him there, and she knew she was entitled to half of it. Janet's attorney did not want to take the time to research it. Instead he would say, "No, you can't get anything, there's no way to get it. Your husband denies that he has it, so there's nothing that can be done." She would leave his office deflated and defeated. She felt reluctant to complain for fear of ruining a friendship. After her divorce was final, she felt even more frustrated, because she knew he had been inadequate and she had not taken responsibility for herself. She had failed to stand up for herself.

This time in your life is stressful enough. Do not do as Janet did. Think twice before using a friend. Your divorce *must* be handled in a businesslike manner.

Remember, it's your life and it's your business.

Making an Educated Choice

- Get referrals. Ask your divorced friends who their attorneys were. If your friends do not feel they got a good settlement, ask them who their *husbands'* attorneys were. You can also get recommendations from acquaintances at your church or work or women's groups of which you are a member. As a last resort, look in the yellow pages of your local telephone book for names of the attorneys who specialize in divorce.
- Consider an attorney who specializes in family law or one who has handled many divorce cases. At this time in your life,

it is most important to have an attorney who "cares," one who wants to get the maximum amount for you and not for himself.

- Make sure you feel comfortable with your attorney. You should not feel inhibited about asking questions. If you do not understand something, ask. It is your divorce.
- Find out who will actually handle your divorce. Will it be given to someone else in the firm—someone with less experience?
- Ask if you will be able to call him or her when you need answers.
- Will he or she be willing to go back to court after the final decree if additional assets are discovered?
- Use the same lawyer as your husband *only* if you have been married a short period of time, have no children, have about the same income and there are no assets to divide.
- Ask the attorney for names of his clients that you can call for references.

See chapter 9 for additional information on choosing an attorney.

Working With Your Attorney

Generally, your initial interview with an attorney will be free, but ask before you make the appointment. Begin, now, to never assume anything.

For many of you, this may be the first time you have been in an attorney's office, and you may be nervous. You must remind yourself that this person is going to work for you and you are there to interview him or her to do a job for you.

First, ask about the divorce laws in your state; this will give you an idea of what to expect. Divorce cases take between two to eighteen months, depending on the state laws and the complexity of your divorce.

You must read and understand everything about your divorce. If you do not, ask your attorney to explain it. Never sign or agree to anything until you understand it fully. You may think that because your lawyer has prepared it, it must be correct. *Not necessarily.* Your attorney is human and can make mistakes. If your attorney seems aggravated by having to explain, then change attorneys. Once again, remember that your attorney works for you, and it is his or her job to help you understand. You must take responsibility for your own life and your lawyer's mistakes.

Once you have chosen a lawyer, do not think your job is done. It has just begun. An attorney is only as good and effective as the information you give him or her. He or she cannot be expected to know and remember every aspect of your life. You are the one who was married to your husband, not the attorney. If you have chosen a successful attorney, he or she has many cases going on, so *it is up to you to get this divorce.* You must totally focus on this part of your life, *now*—as if it were a business—because you can rest assured that your husband is treating it like a business. It is crucial that you remember this. You *must* think ahead of the attorneys, *you must think for them*, and then you must remind them! Supply as much information as you can. Keep a pad of paper on your bedside table to write down ideas during those sleepless nights. Do not think you will remember it in the morning. Give each idea, in writing, to your attorney, and keep a copy for yourself...things get lost.

Because of the state of mind Barbara was in during her divorce, all she wanted to do was put everything in the hands of her attorney and say, "Now get my divorce." However, he had other clients and other cases. She had to stay on top of the case daily and constantly feed him information (and still the divorce took nearly a year). While your attorney may be interested and concerned, he or she cannot be nearly as interested and concerned as you.

Most importantly, be completely truthful with your attorney. He or she needs to know everything—but do not expect your attorney to be your therapist. He or she is dealing with the legal matters while you have to deal with the family matters.

SURVIVAL TIP

Never fail to discuss with your attorney, no matter how embarrassing, the events that occurred during the marriage that resulted in personal harm or humiliation. The reason for this is that those types of harm, in some states, can result in a monetary award favorable to you or at least an enhancement of your settlement.

We know you are completely exhausted, but you will have time to rest when this is over. Now is not the time to rest.

Using a Mediator

You might choose to use a mediator. In other words, you and your spouse talk to a person trained to listen and help resolve any disputes. A mediator might be a retired judge or a lawyer, but in any event, a person specially trained in mediation. Mediation is fine if you and your spouse are able to communicate. You will sit down with the mediator and thereafter he or she will help you work out the settlement. Mediation can save you money. However, I urge you to be very careful, especially if you have a domineering or controlling husband who may turn the mediation sessions into his own forum for wife bashing.

Fees

Get in writing how you will be charged and what those charges will cover. There are usually four options to consider:

Hourly fee. Money charged per hour worked. It is the most common fee arrangement. Get estimates on each part of your case and demand regular written progress reports.

Retainer. Money that an attorney wants up front. You retain him with a certain amount of money. It is like a deposit and is credited toward your monthly bills. Make sure a retainer is refundable and is, in fact, credited against time spent on your case.

Flat fee. You and your attorney agree on a flat fee and the fee will not change. Inquire as to how expenses are handled.

Range fee. Attorney leaves the final fee open, not knowing how much work will be needed on your case. You are given a range (example: between $1,000 and $5,000) of what you will pay.

We suggest that you ask for an itemized bill each month so that you will be able to stay on top of things. Ask for an explanation of anything that does not sound reasonable or that you do not understand. You will probably be required to sign a written agreement with your lawyer. Know what it says and, if you are in doubt, demand answers before you sign. Remember, you are a consumer of services, and the lawyer is working for you.

After you have chosen a lawyer, you will find that getting divorced entails just three steps. Simply put, they are:

Separation. When you and your husband live apart before the divorce is final.

Division of assets. When you and your husband put into writing how the children, assets, and liabilities will be divided.

Finalization of divorce. When you and your husband and your attorneys go through the actual divorce proceedings.

THE SEPARATION

The first step toward divorce is the separation. It is the time you spend apart from your spouse before you get your divorce. The amount of time varies from state to state.

Perhaps the time you are separated preceding the divorce is the first time you have ever lived alone. You went from your family home to school to life with a husband. This may be the first time you have taken care of the bills, or made career and investment decisions. Perhaps it is the first time you have been completely in charge of your life.

If it is possible to stay where you were living while you were married, do so. It makes it easier if you do not have to move out right away.

Your separation will be a time of learning, of finding out things you can do without, of dividing your property. You may find that living alone is something you love better than anything! Spend this time getting used to being alone. Determine what you want to do with the rest of your life. Do not rush—take one day at a time.

Use your separation time to read books and articles about things you need to know about your new life and your divorce. Do not wallow in self-pity. Try to be positive in your conversations with your friends. Act better than you feel and you will actually start to feel better.

If you have not worked outside of the home before your divorce, your lawyer may tell you not to get a job because it will be used to lower your settlement potential. Your attorney may tell you that even taking a computer course can be used to prove that you do not need financial help. This will be a subject that you need to discuss completely with your attorney, because you may really feel the need to get a job or take a class, for the sake of your mental health, social contact, or reassurance of your self-sufficiency. However, take the advice of your attorney, and, whatever the decision, use this time wisely. Make plans. Do not just sit.

You do not have to spend your separation devising statements about why you want a divorce. "No fault" divorce means that you do not have to blame him and he does not have to blame you in order for a divorce to take place. However, should your divorce be settled in front of a judge and some fault is brought up, even though it may be a no-fault divorce, what you have done may actually have some bearing on the case and your potential settlement.

Temporary Support

BARBARA: *My main concern when I filed for divorce was how I would live. I thought the money would end immediately and I would be destitute. I did not realize I could go to court and demand and receive temporary support.*

My attorney told me to calculate the amount of money I needed monthly to pay all my expenses. This should include the house payment, utilities, insurance premiums, etc. (a work-sheet is included in this chapter). My attorney said, "Don't cut yourself short. Write down everything it takes to run a house-hold, including the things you had before filing for the divorce, such as a housekeeper, gardener, dry cleaning, and entertain-ment. When we go to court, your husband and his attorney may try to insist we cut it, so don't start at rock bottom. However, don't write anything down if you can't prove the need."

This was the first time we went to court, and much to my surprise I received an award of temporary support. My hus-band was horrified because he had to come up with the support payment each month. One of the problems we had in our marriage was that he would often let months go by before he paid the bills. Now I received the monthly temporary support and I was able to pay bills when they were due.

When my husband declared bankruptcy during our divorce proceedings, I thought I was in a bind. We had to go back to court because he wanted to cut my temporary support, but the court did not let him.

If you are filing for temporary support, the worksheet on page 28-29 might assist you in calculating your needs.

Getting Your Economic Life in Order

Get credit where credit is due! One of the first things Bar-bara's attorney suggested was that she get a credit card in her own name. It is most important that you use your legal name, Sarah Jones—not Mrs. Fred Jones. Mrs. Fred Jones is a social title, not a legal name. Your legal name might be your first name plus your maiden (birth) name, or your first name, maiden name, and married last name.

You can even revert to your maiden name easily if you wish.

As long as you keep the same social security number, the legal system does not have a problem with the last name you choose to use. You do go to court to have it done, though, but it can be done at the time of your divorce.

Establishing a Line of Credit

Another thing you should do immediately is establish a line of credit. Get a loan in your own name from a bank and pay it back in a timely fashion so a bank will know that you are a good risk. You may feel reluctant, as Barbara did, to pay interest, but it is important because should an emergency occur someday where you need money quickly, you will have established a line of credit. You have to pledge collateral (some kind of property to leave with the bank) until the loan is paid off. But it still belongs to you, it's just pledged.

Barbara's attorney helped her by picking up the phone and calling a banker.

"I'm sending Barbara Jowell over to you," he said. "Can you fix her up with a small loan? Good. At one percent over prime? Great. Thanks."

BARBARA: *When I got to the bank, the arrangements had already been started. In no time the banker had loan papers ready for me to sign.*

"Here you go, Barbara," the banker said. "I've taken care of everything. And that's at two percent over prime."

In the past I would have accepted the higher percentage rate, silently assuming the banker must have changed his mind. But I was feeling strong and confident, the result of asserting myself and filing for divorce.

"Two percent over prime?" I smiled as I looked him in the eye. "I understood my attorney to say one percent."

"Oh, well, of course," he said, "it's one percent."

As easy as that. A small challenge faced boosted my confidence beyond measure.

I put the loan right into a savings account. Then I used that money to pay back the loan. Yes, I had to pay some interest on the loan, but the amount was small and I was also making interest on the money in the savings account! The entire transaction gave me credit in my own name, and a good credit record with the bank.

Barbara was fortunate that her attorney was willing to make these arrangements, but it is something that you can do all by yourself. If you do not have collateral, you will need to discuss with your attorney what the effect of getting a job would have on your divorce proceeding. If your attorney says that it is all right, then find a job...any kind of a job. Obtaining a job will show that you are willing to work in order to establish some credit history and have the money to pay off a loan in order to establish a line of credit. (See chapter 10 for additional information on establishing credit.)

TEMPORARY SUPPORT WORKSHEET

Monthly Expenses

Housing:	1. Rent/house payment	$_____
	2. Insurance	_____
	3. Maintenance, repair, service	_____
	4. Utilities (gas, water, electric)	_____
	5. Telephone	_____
Auto and	1. Car payments	_____
Transportation:	2. Insurance	_____
	3. Gasoline and oil	_____
	4. Maintenance and repair	_____
	5. Mass transit/taxi service/parking	_____
	6. Air travel	_____
Insurance:	1. Life	_____
	2. Health, hospitalization	_____
	3. Other	_____
Food:	1. Groceries	_____
	2. Meals out	_____
Medical:	1. Doctors	_____
(not covered	2. Dentists	_____
by insurance)	3. Drugs	_____

Education:	School supplies, fees, etc.	_____
Personal:	1. Grooming (barber, hairdresser)	_____
	2. Clothing	_____
	3. Cleaning and laundry	_____
	4. Housekeeper expenses	_____
	5. Clothes alterations	_____
Entertainment:	Movies, concerts, etc.	_____
Dues:	Clubs, organizations	_____
Other:	1. Subscriptions/dues	_____
	2. Charitable donations, church	_____
	3. Taxes	_____
	4. Postage	_____
Children:	1. School lunches	_____
	2. Orthodontic care	_____
	3. School tuition	_____
	4. School supplies	_____
	5. Childrens' activities	_____
	6. Child care/babysitters	_____

TOTAL $_____

Monthly Income

Petitioner (you)
   Salary $_____
   Other Income   _____

TOTAL INCOME $_____

Monthly Income

Respondent (your husband) $_____

DIVIDING THE ASSETS

The next step is to ascertain how much money you and your husband have and how much is owed. Only then will you have a clear picture of what you and he will divide.

Just by reading this book, it is obvious that you are getting a grip on your divorce. You are taking steps to deal with your loss. No one else can read this for you, and no one else will react to it exactly as you will. There is logic in your life, and you are doing the right thing by learning about it.

You must remember you have an investment of x amount of years in your marriage. Although you may have been "just" a mother or "just" a wife, you have been, at least, an equal partner, and you are about to dissolve a partnership. If this had been a business partnership, would you be content to walk away and give your half of the partnership to your partner?

If your spouse earned the money, remember, you *saved* the money by providing a home, raising children, and taking care of all the things that have to be done in a home. Do you know how much these services would have cost your partner over the years, had you not been there to provide them? *Never* say I was "just" anything! Be proud of what you are and what you have done. Do not ever let your spouse convince you that what you do or have done is not important.

While searching for an attorney, even if you were never a wage earner during your marriage, do not sell yourself short. You deserve the best attorney you can find. Do not make hasty decisions or let anyone rush you when negotiating a settlement.

No matter how cold and calculating this sounds, just remember, even when you think you are economically ready for divorce, you probably are not. One of our purposes in writing this book is to help you avoid the disadvantages most women suffer in divorce.

On your first visit to an attorney, it would be nice to be able to take a list of all the family assets and liabilities. However, if you have never known about family finances, do not panic. It is your attorney's job to ferret out that information. The best way to find the family assets and liabilities is to look on your income tax return and financial statements. Everything is listed. Every cent, every asset, and every liability you and your husband have must be there. (Unless he has cheated on the income tax return, but assume for the time being that he would not stoop that low.)

The important thing to remember is that *the tax return is yours as much as his.* Even if you did not help prepare it, you signed it and you are entitled to the information that is on it.

Do not be embarrassed if you do not remember what is on the tax return. Sad but true—many women in top-level executive positions sign their tax returns without reading them.

How can you get the income tax return if your husband is reluctant to give it to you? First, check the files at your house. If you have access to his office, check there. If you cannot find it, call the accountant or tax preparer who prepared the return and ask for a copy. If necessary, write to the IRS for a copy. It takes longer from the IRS, but they will send it to you.

What if you cannot read the income tax return? Go to see a bookkeeper or an accountant and say, "Tell me in plain language what this means." The return will show any stocks and bonds, your husband's income, any liabilities and debts. Do not panic if you cannot find everything you need. Your lawyer can subpoena the records and get sworn statements from your husband and his tax preparers if necessary.

What Gets Divided?

- All assets acquired during marriage whether in his name, your name, or both. This includes the house, money in the bank, securities, furniture, furnishings, cars, pension plans, insurance, retirement plans, and IRA and Keogh funds.
- In community property states, property of the marriage is generally divided 50-50 in no-fault divorces. Those states include California, Louisiana, Washington, Arizona, Texas, Nevada, New Mexico, Wisconsin, and Idaho.
- Practices regarding the dividing up of the assets vary from state to state. It may depend on the duration of the marriage, your ages, your needs and earning power, prior marriages, children, financial and homemaking contributions, and customary standard of living. You must check and understand completely your state laws. You can find this information in your public library, or your attorney will be able to tell you.
- Both parties are entitled to be informed of all the family assets. A settlement may be set aside later if it turns out that significant information was withheld or falsified.

What Is Not Included?

Assets of any kind you or your husband had before marriage. If it was yours before you took the vows, it is yours to take away after the divorce. However, if an item belonged to one spouse before marriage and was sold after the marriage and used to purchase a joint asset, the proceeds from the sale would remain separate property but the interest or dividends from the joint asset would be the property of both spouses. This includes stocks, bonds, special accounts, houses, cars, coin collections.

- Anything you or he received as an inheritance, a gift to you individually, or money you were paid from personal injury settlements. For instance, if you inherited your family's land, it is separate property and will not be divided in the divorce. However, if the two of you jointly purchased the land, he is entitled to a share of that land, in an amount, generally, equivalent to what he put into it.

SURVIVAL TIP

Be aware of whether or not your husband has a pension plan, because many times the pension plan is one of the most valuable assets that you will divide.

Finding the Pension Plan

Ann decided to use a close friend as her divorce attorney. For the time they were in the attorney-client relationship, she decided she would act like his partner rather than a client. Yes, he was a friend and she felt sure he had her best interests at heart. She also knew she needed to help him all she could, and it was another way of taking control of her own life. After all, she knew more about her life than he did, even though he was a longtime friend.

Ann's husband declared bankruptcy during their divorce. Because the large national company he worked for had loaned him a great deal of money several years prior to the divorce, the bankruptcy naturally wiped out his debt to the large company. Supposedly, he gave the large company his pension to cover their loss, since he wanted to continue to work for them. He stated to his attorney that Ann would not receive half of the pension plan to which she was legally entitled.

Since 1974 a series of laws called the Employee Retirement Income Securities Act (ERISA) has gradually mandated a spouse's right to share in a pension fund.

Ann did not believe her husband had surrendered his pension plan. Knowing her husband as she did, she knew the pension plan was still there, but she and her attorney could get no cooperation from the company or her husband. When the divorce became final, the lawyer wrote words and phrases into the settlement that saved her. The property settlement stated that if anything was discovered that had been hidden, Ann would have the right to claim it all.

Ann and her attorney agreed that each year at the anniversary of the divorce they would contact the company to see if the pension had been reinstated. On the first anniversary, Ann asked her attorney to write a letter to the company asking if the pension payments had been reinstated...no response. A month later she asked him to write again...and again, no response. Ann's attorney suggested that she occasionally call the company to see if she could get any response. For six months she called. Finally, one day she talked to a man who did not realize that he was telling her something the company and her former husband had rather he not. Ann asked if the pension had been reinstated. The man said her former husband had always received his monthly benefits, that they had never been interrupted. He did not understand what the confusion was about.

Ann sued her former husband and the very large national company and won. She now receives a lifetime monthly payment and she also recovered the eighteen months of payments that she had not received plus all her attorney fees.

If you truly believe something, do not let your attorney or anyone talk you out of it and do not ever give up. Many times you will have to strongly encourage your attorney to pursue your wishes, but take control and remember, *he works for you! Take responsibility for your own life—no one is supposed to take care of you but you.*

The Tax Man's Share

If there are assets to be divided, your attorney or accountant must be able to advise you about any tax issues that arise. If they do not know the answers to your tax questions, insist that they get the answers for you. For example:

Alimony (spousal support). Taxable to the recipient, a deduction to the spouse.

Child support. The custodial parent will legally be able to take the tax deduction for each child. The parent who receives the child support does not have to pay taxes on the payments.

The family home. Who will get it? Should it be kept or sold? What is it worth? If the house has increased in value, there can result a large tax to the seller.

In just these three instances, you can see the good sense of having competent tax advice. Make sure you understand the consequences of all tax issues. It is not enough that your attorney understands—you must understand also. He or she will not have to pay the tax, you will. Again, remember, the attorney works for you. It is his or her duty to help you understand everything. Take charge; ultimately, it is all up to you.

TAKING CARE OF THE CHILDREN

No matter how you feel about your spouse, keep the best interests of your children in mind. They did not cause this divorce, and they should not suffer because of the way you feel about your husband. If you and your husband can communicate about the children, then try to work out the arrangements for them together *with their well-being in mind.* Try not to have to settle this issue in court, because chances are that neither of you will be happy with what the court decides.

Child custody has changed in recent years. Custody is no longer automatically awarded to the mother. Both of you will most likely have to work outside the home after the divorce, and it will have to be determined who best can take care of the children and still hold down a job.

You will have some very serious decisions to make about your children. Although custody can be changed, it requires legal steps. Discuss the question of child custody very carefully with your attorney, and be sure you understand every angle completely before agreeing to anything. Be aware that your spouse may threaten to seek custody of the children in order to force you to make a quick and smaller financial settlement.

Although terms and conditions vary state by state, some of the main issues to be settled regarding children are:

Child Custody

Temporary custody. The child lives with either you or your husband while the divorce proceedings are going on. (If you want the child/children to live with you, do not leave them with your husband when you separate, because the court will usually award temporary custody to the parent with whom they are living at the time of the court order.)

Permanent custody. This is the decision as to where the children's primary home will be when the divorce is final: where they will live, go to school, what church they will attend, etc. Legal custody can be handled either as joint or sole custody:

- *Joint legal custody.* Both you and your spouse make the decisions about your children's lives together. This is the very best situation for the child if you and your spouse can put your differences aside and agree to do what is "in the best interest of the children."
- *Sole custody.* Either you or your husband alone will make all the decisions about your children's lives after the divorce is final.

Child Support

Who pays? The non-custodial parent pays a certain amount periodically (usually monthly) to the custodial parent.

How much? This amount is usually established by the court or by the various state legislatures. Talk to your lawyer and have him or her explain to you the range of support you should expect to receive. Naturally it is best if the parents can agree on an amount before going to court. Make sure that your agreement allows for an increase. Remember that unexpected things will come up, such as braces for teeth, etc.

How long? The normal time is until the child is eighteen years old or graduates from high school, whichever is later. A parent most likely has no obligation to support a child once he or she reaches the age of eighteen years in most states. Attempt to agree that the husband will help the children until they graduate from college, in a reasonable amount of time.

ALIMONY (SPOUSAL SUPPORT)

Alimony may be paid in addition to the division of property. Keep that in mind when seeking it. Most states allow for it, but in other states it can only be authorized by an agreement between the parties.

Alimony today is designed to be temporary rather than permanent and is awarded according to the individual circumstances of the people involved. A young mother with preschool children may be awarded alimony until the children reach school age. Also, spousal support may be awarded a young mother in order for her to attend school and ultimately keep her "off welfare." An older woman who had never worked outside the home might be awarded alimony until she is capable of self-support in some manner.

Alimony is based on the length of time the marriage endured, ability of the paying spouse to make the payments, standard of living of both partners, earning abilities, health, etc. One thing about spousal support is that you should never count on getting it. If you do get it, it can always be modified at a later date if the circumstances of either party change. My only advice is, always try! Nothing ventured, nothing gained.

SURVIVAL TIP

If you gave up attending college to work in order for your husband to go to college to get a professional degree, you may be able to get ongoing support because you own part of his degree.

It might even be given to the husband if he earns less than his wife. In a recent case, a woman who made a six-figure salary with a publishing company married a man who had two teenage daughters. His salary from a nonprofit organization was considerably less. After they had a child of their own and she took a second mortgage on her home to pay off his debt, she found he had been unfaithful and she filed for divorce. In the settlement, it was decreed that she must pay him alimony. So, ladies, do not count on alimony—you may end up having to pay him!

SOCIAL SECURITY AFTER DIVORCE

As a divorced spouse, a woman is eligible for the same social security benefits she would get if she were still married—a sum equal to half her ex-husband's check if he is still alive, or to the full amount if he has died—provided that:

- They were married at least ten years.
- She is not currently married to someone else.
- She did not earn enough on the job to be eligible for a benefit equal to or greater than his.
- He has filed for benefits, or else she is over age sixty-two and they have been divorced for more than two years. (The two-year waiting period is waived if she is over age sixty-two and he was entitled to benefits before their divorce.)

Her benefit does not affect his. Similarly, if he has remarried, his second wife's benefit does not affect the first wife. If the first wife was married for at least ten years to someone else after her first marriage (which also lasted at least ten years), and is now divorced a second time, she can choose whether she wants to apply on the first husband's account or the second husband's account.

FINALIZING THE DIVORCE

Most cases are settled out of court, and we suggest that if at all possible, settle your divorce and leave a judge out of it. If you do find that you must go to trial, then go quickly down to the divorce court and watch a case in order to understand what happens.

You will find that it does not matter who is right or wrong, the judge will divide the assets according to the laws in the state where you live, and usually neither side is any more satisfied than if they had come to an agreement in their attorneys' offices or through mediation. Most women who have had their case settled in the courtroom felt that their lives had been spread before the entire city and that they had no more secrets— especially if they had a particularly vindictive spouse.

If you reach a child and property settlement with your spouse through your attorneys, then your court day will be just a formality. At the time of Barbara's divorce, she had no idea when it was close to becoming final. Her attorney just called her one afternoon and asked if she was "ready to get this divorce finalized." When she answered, "Yes," he said they could go to court the next morning. They arrived with a signed settlement agreement. The judge asked if they were satisfied with the settlement; they replied they were, and that was it. Divorced. It probably took fifteen minutes. It's relatively easy if you work everything out before you go before the judge.

BARBARA: *Now, I was ready for the rest of my life. As I mentioned earlier, I felt relief when my marriage was over and the divorce was final. The only problem was, I was terrified for my financial security. I had not worked for pay for twenty-five years, and I had a great deal of fear and anxiety over how to support myself. And "all" I had done in the twenty-five years of my marriage was "just" be a volunteer in the community.*

However, I was fortunate to have a very wise friend who helped me to see and understand what those volunteer skills were worth. I could take my volunteer skills in fund-raising and turn them into a career. There are organizations that are willing to pay for all of that knowledge and work that I had been doing for free for twenty-five years.

After my divorce, I was working. I had my own salary. I knew I could go on with my own hopes and dreams. I realized I had more financial security than I had ever had when I was married. Why? Because I did not have to worry about what my husband was spending anymore. I just had to worry about me, and I could control me.

Alone now, I am in control of my life and my financial future. You will be also.

Remember, divorce is not just an end, it's also a beginning.

3

Widowed

DONNETTE: *I wish I could reach out and take your hand now. You have just suffered one of the most significant losses of your lifetime. You have just lost your husband. You didn't plan it to be this way. Your husband has died, and if you're feeling like I did, you're feeling overwhelmed—with sadness and fear for what the future will bring.*

Please believe these words: You will make it through this, *and when you do, you will have discovered strengths you never knew you had.*

Immediately upon the death of your husband, *call your closest friend or relative to come be with you.* Close friends were with Donnette every moment—at the hospital, at home, spending the night before family arrived to be in the house with her. Your friends want to help in any way they can.

A personal note here. If you were not present when your husband died, you may wish to view the body. Mac collapsed at the YMCA. He died before Donnette arrived at the hospital. She requested to see him before the body was transported to the funeral home. In regard to viewing the body, do what feels right to you at the time.

THE FUNERAL ARRANGEMENTS

If your husband died in the hospital, the hospital will ask you which undertaker you wish to use. The hospital will call the funeral home of your choice and arrange for the body to be transferred.

If your husband died at home, *you* will need to contact the funeral home. Some states require that a physician or designated public official pronounce death before the body can be transferred to the funeral home. Your funeral home or local hospice can advise you as to the requirements of your state and whom to contact to legally pronounce death.

If the funeral is to be held in another town, the undertaker in that city must be contacted. That funeral home will transport or arrange for transportation of the body.

Ask a friend or family member to accompany you to the funeral home to discuss the service and costs. *Get the costs in writing.* Most undertakers are honest and compassionate; however, it is your responsibility to stay within your funeral budget.

Be sure to request the following items:

- Registration pad for friends who come to your home and the funeral home.
- Registration pad for food brought by friends.
- Registration pad for listing flowers.
- Outline for information needed in the obituary.
- Certified copies of the death certificate. Order fifteen. Extra copies may be obtained later for a slight fee, from the county clerk's office.

Type of Service

Perhaps your spouse has indicated the type of disposition and type of service he wishes. If not, these will be your decisions.

- Check to see if there is an organ donor designation on his driver's license.
- You may choose to have the service that is customary within your religious preference, or you may choose to have the

service at the funeral home. You may decide to have a graveside service only.

- You will need to decide whether you want a public service, with friends and business associates attending, or a private service, for family only.
- You may wish to have a public memorial service followed by a private graveside service for family and close friends only.

Flowers and Memorials

- Decide whether to have flowers at the funeral. You will need to indicate this in the obituary.
- Decide whether to indicate a specific charity or charities for memorials. This will also be indicated in the obituary.

SURVIVAL TIP

Take advantage of all the services of your funeral home. They can supply you with forms that will help you remember all the kindnesses people have done for you.

Notifying Others of His Death

It will be your task to notify friends, family, and your husband's employer. You will also have to choose the pallbearers. Some funeral homes will notify pallbearers for you.

You will probably want to prepare the obituary to be sent to the local newspapers. If the funeral home does not have an outline or form to help you with preparation of the obituary, ask for help from a funeral home employee.

You might want to ask a close friend to help you do the following:

- Notify other friends.
- Arrange for care of young children.
- Take care of arrangements for out-of-town friends and family.
- Manage the registration of friends who come to the home or funeral home to offer condolences. Most funeral homes sup-

ply registration forms for this purpose. Order announcements and thank-you cards to be printed.

- Manage the listing of food and flowers.
- For at least a week after the obituary appears in the newspaper, arrange to have someone stay in the house during times you cannot be there. This is especially important during the time of the funeral. Police advised Donnette that burglaries often occur when it has been publicized that a house could be unoccupied at a certain time (such as in an obituary stating the time of a funeral).

SETTLING THE ESTATE

"I don't know where to begin. I look at everything on my desk and know I need to start somewhere—but where?" Carolyn's lament a couple of days after the funeral is typical. She is actually an organized, get-it-done-yesterday type of person. She feels disoriented and confused from exhaustion, grief, and all the busy work of the funeral.

If you're feeling the way Carolyn did, here's a checklist that will help you feel more organized. If you are the executor of your husband's estate, you may find that some of these duties will be included in the executor's list as well. If you are not the executor, work with her or him closely so that you are not duplicating each other's efforts. You may want to check off items as you accomplish them.

CHECKLIST FOR WIDOWS

___1.   Open a bank account in your own name, if you do not already have one. (If you are executor for your husband's will, you will open a separate account for the estate. (See the "Duties of Executor" checklist, page 48, item 8.)

___2.   Notify your bank and all insurance companies, including life, homeowner, and auto. It may take a few weeks for life insurance proceeds to be paid. Some life insurance benefits are hand-delivered by insurance company representatives who will make a pitch to get you to invest the benefits with their company. Do not make hasty decisions. Discuss all investments carefully with your chosen advisor or financial planner. Chapter 9, "The Professionals You Work With: Who, What, When, Where, and How," tells you how to go about choosing your advisers. If you are not sure that you have located all life insurance policies, consider all places where your husband could have purchased life insurance: clubs, banks, fraternities, credit life insurance on loans, and alumnae associations.

___3.   Contact the attorney who will probate the will. If you are comfortable using the attorney who drew up your husband's will, he or she would be the logical one to guide the estate through probate. However, if that attorney also represents your husband's business and there is a potential conflict of interest between the estate and your husband's business, then you will need to choose a different attorney.

The probate process authenticates your husband's will, appoints the executor and issues "letters testamentary," which are documents that attest to the fact that the executor may legally act on behalf of the estate. Under the probate process, the executor will pay your husband's outstanding debts, file federal and state taxes on his estate, and distribute assets to the heirs in accordance with his will. Even if there is a living trust, much of the process described above has to be followed.

You will need to supply an inventory of all assets and debts during the probate process. The more details you can take care of yourself, the less you will pay in legal fees. You will want to volunteer to do as much as you can to keep legal fees down. Always get a fee estimate.

Be leery of agreeing to pay a percentage of the estate to the lawyer. It is generally preferable to pay an hourly fee as agreed between you and your attorney.

___4. If you apply for a family allowance at probate court, then you will need to estimate your monthly living expenses for this purpose. Many attorneys advise that you use your check register and average the last six months' living expenses to arrive at your monthly living expenses.

___5. If you do not have a credit card in your own name, you may wish to establish as much credit as possible in your own name before notifying credit card companies of your mate's death. It is against the law for your credit cards to be canceled just because you have become widowed, but if your credit was based on your husband's earning power and was in his name only, you may be called upon to reapply and receive lower credit limits.

___6. Review credit card agreements. Determine if you have credit card insurance coverage. If your husband's death was accidental, some credit cards have accidental death coverage.

___7. Notify all retirement plan administrators of your husband's death.

___8. Call the Veterans Administration if your husband was a veteran. Ask for VA pamphlet 27-82-2, *A Summary of Veterans Administration Benefits*.

___9. Go to the Social Security office and file for benefits. Funeral benefits are small, but each dollar helps.

___10. Check with your legal counsel before you change the title on any joint assets.

___11. Do not pay any debts that are not your responsibility. When in doubt, check with your attorney. Work closely with the executor of the estate.

___12. Revise your own will. (See chapter 10, "Protecting Your Assets.")

Administering the Estate

If your husband made a will, he will have probably named someone to carry out, or execute, the terms of the will. Such a person is called an executor.

It is the duty of the executor to administer the estate according to the letter and spirit of the laws of the state to the best of his or her information and ability. The executor owes certain very high duties to those whom he or she serves. Those duties include a strict loyalty to and impartiality among all the persons interested in the estate. The executor must act with utmost good faith and avoid any conflict between his or her personal interest and that of the estate or the legatees (persons to whom property is given by the will.) In almost every state, the administration of an estate involves at least four areas of activity:

- The assets and property your husband owned at the time of his death are identified.
- Your husband's creditors are notified of his death and the debts of and claims against him are paid out of his assets and property.
- All tax returns required of your husband or his estate are filed, and all taxes owed are paid in full.
- Your husband's remaining assets and property are distributed to the legatees (inheritors) who are entitled to them under his will.

The executor is not the owner of the property of the estate. Generally (and in some states along with the probate court), the executor is the temporary caretaker of the property of the estate. The property of the estate must be cared for as a prudent person would care for his or her own property. Under some circumstances, for instance, an executor may be required to carry on a farm, ranch, factory, or other business which the decedent (the deceased person) owned or had an interest in at the time of the death. In many states, an executor's power to sell and convey property exists only if it is granted expressly by the terms of the will and allowed by state law, or if the sale is necessary for purposes of administration, such as to raise money to pay claims or taxes.

Commingling of Property. One of the most important duties of the executor is *not to commingle* (or mix) property and funds of the estate with his or her personal funds or property. If in doubt, the executor should check with the attorney or accountant for the estate about establishing bank accounts and procedures to help assure that this does not occur.

Distribution of Estate. When the executor has completed administration of the estate, he or she has the duty to distribute it to the persons who are designated by the will. Most states have a specified period of time by which claims against the estate must be presented (say, six months), and the distribution may not take place prior to this designated time. In those states in which death tax returns are required, it may be much longer before the estate can be distributed.

In most states, it is required that a final accounting to the legatees be distributed at the time of the distribution of the estate. Even when not required, this communication is a good idea. In prolonged administrations, it is a good idea to furnish an annual accounting to all persons interested in the estate.

SURVIVAL TIP

It is essential for the executor to communicate regularly with all persons interested in the estate about the course of the administration of the estate. According to our legal counsel, a main source of conflict in settling an estate is lack of meaningful communication between the executor and the legatees.

If you're not the executor of your husband's estate, he or she is one of the most important persons in your life right now. Here is a list of the executor's duties. *Please don't be overwhelmed by this list.* Remember, the executor has months—even years in some cases—to accomplish these duties.

DUTIES OF EXECUTOR

___1.   Protect assets before probate. For instance, do not allow nephew Jim to take the watch bequeathed to him in the will, prior to the final distribution of property. Once the watch is out of town, it is difficult to get it back for appraisal purposes if later necessary.

___2.   File claims for life insurance, pension plan, profit-sharing, social security, and VA (Veterans Administration) benefits, if applicable. This may be done by a widow or other beneficiary, but the executor needs to be informed of all details and results of these processes.

___3.   Probate will.

___4.   Advertise grant of letters testamentary—advertise for claims against the estate.

___5.   Inventory safe-deposit box.

___6.   File notice of fiduciary relationship with the Internal Revenue Service.

___7.   File for a tax ID number for estate income tax returns.

___8.   Open bank account for estate.

___9.   Obtain income tax returns for the prior three years and all gift tax returns filed. Check past income tax returns for assets. Schedule B lists dividend and interest income, and names any stock, mutual fund, and taxable bond that generated income. Your husband's accountant will have prior income tax returns.

___10.   Obtain values at the date of death on all assets and at six months following date of death if alternate valuation method is to be considered for estate purposes. Values of stocks, bonds, and mutual funds can be obtained by calling your husband's stockbroker, and/or by checking the investment section of your local newspaper. Obtain appraisals on all real and personal property. Obtain comparative financial statements for any closely held businesses. Review the possibility of special valuation farm and business estate. (Work with attorney/accountant.)

___11. Schedule cash needs of the estate. Pay all debts of estate. Review medical bills. Obtain a list of the debts of the deceased. Decide if assets need to be sold. Consider stock redemption under IRC Section 303. (Work with attorney/accountant.)

___12. File final individual income tax returns.

___13. File U.S. estate tax return nine months after date of death, or consider extension.

___14. File fiduciary income tax return after choosing fiscal year end.

___15. Allow for safeguarding of any assets distributed to minors.

___16. Prepare a statement regarding distribution of assets.

___17. Check with your accountant about necessity of:

    A. Notifying officers of S corporations in which your husband owned stock before funding any testamentary trusts that could cause termination of S status.

    B. Notifying any partnership in which your husband held an interest to consider filing a section 754 election to step up the basis of partnership assets.

    C. Considering the QTIP (Qualified Terminal Interest Property) election.

If He Died Intestate

If a person does not have a will, the state provides a will for him or her. If your husband died without a will, the probate court will appoint a representative to handle the details of settling of his estate. The laws of the state where you live will determine what you and your family will inherit. It will be to your benefit to work closely with this person and handle as much of the detail work as possible.

GRIEF FROM A WIDOW'S POINT OF VIEW

DONNETTE: *As I mentioned in the Preface, I was happily married to a good-looking forty-nine-year-old attorney whose second bypass surgery had been deemed highly successful. He was back to jogging five to six miles a day and loved sailing on the weekends. Mac was my companion. He took care of me.*

Mac dropped dead after a workout at the YMCA. Six months prior to Mac's death, when I first learned of his need for a second bypass surgery, I could have put my fist through a wall. I was mad at the world, at God and everybody. We already had been through one bypass surgery—why another one? I was just livid. Mac had done everything he was supposed to—jogged, worked out faithfully, hadn't eaten saturated fat in years. After his second bypass surgery, something came over me—a sense of peace and acceptance—and my anger went away. From then on, I was grateful for every day I had with him. As it turned out, I had only six more months.

So when Mac died, I had already experienced much of the anger stage of grief.

When you are widowed, you can expect to experience normal, predictable stages of grief: (1) shock/denial, (2) anger/depression—accompanied at times by other issues such as guilt and fear of imposing—and finally, (3) acceptance.

As miserable as you are during the grieving process, please realize that you need to take time to work through the stages of grief. No one suffers these stages in exactly the same manner or in exactly the same time frame. You will be healthier later if you allow yourself to grieve now.

Shock/Denial

In the first stage of grief, you may experience shock and denial when you first learn that he may die—or when he dies—or at both times. You may feel disorientation, forgetfulness, sleeplessness, nausea, or loss of appetite. You may feel isolated from the rest of the world, or you may wonder why you feel compelled to do weird things. "Am I crazy?" is a question we often hear from those who have just suffered the death of a loved one.

According to Mark Mercer, M.S., LPC, a hospice counselor, many people who are grieving question their sanity.

"First, bereaved persons have often reported some strange experiences—hearing the voice of the person who has died, feeling a sense of their actual presence, or even seeing them vividly either while sleeping or waking," Mercer says. "These are common experiences of grieving people, but they can add to the feelings of isolation and the fear of losing their mind.

"Grieving people make statements like, 'I don't know where to start, what I'm saying doesn't make sense.' It's reassuring when they hear, 'You don't have to make sense. Just tell me what you're feeling.'

"And it relieves the feeling of 'being crazy' to get permission to do things that to others may seem irrational. I remember a young man whose fiancée had died suddenly while he was in the hospital. No one had told him, because they hadn't wanted to upset him while he was ill. After being discharged from the hospital, he discovered that his wife-to-be was dead and the funeral and burial were already over.

"He spent hours, daily, at the cemetery, until friends became worried and told him this was excessive, that he should get on with his life.

"When he met with me, I told him to visit the grave for as long and as often as he wanted to. Within two weeks the cemetery visits had become shorter and less frequent. But he had needed the permission to immerse himself in the reality of death. Otherwise, the feelings of unreality, or craziness, could have lasted for years.

"This feeling of unreality about death, so typical of the early weeks of grief, can be a very distressing experience. Other people seem to be going about their business as though nothing out of the ordinary has happened. Grieving people may describe a sense of being locked inside some sort of bubble, alone with

their feelings of sadness and devastation. They feel completely
out of sync with the 'normal' world carrying on all around them.
This bizarre, out-of-touch sensation can make them feel even
sadder (and crazier) when the outside world is filled with joyful
sights and sounds.

"Fortunately, even though it may seem to take forever, it may
be helpful for newly grieving persons to remind themselves, 'I'm
not crazy, I'm just grieving.'"

Anger/Depression

As different as the two emotions of anger and depression are,
you may find yourself swinging between them. You may be
angry that your husband is gone—angry with the doctor, the
hospital, and God. Within a short time you might plunge into
such deep despair and fear, you don't know if you'll ever be able
to overcome it. Perhaps you were angry, as Donnette was, when
you learned your husband might die, so you're not feeling anger
so strongly now that he is gone because you've already experienced that stage of grief. Or maybe you're feeling that anger
more strongly than ever. As much as it hurts to allow yourself
these feelings of anger and intense sadness as you are coping
with the endless details of settling the estate, comforting children, and making financial decisions, these feelings are an
essential part of your ultimate healing.

Now, what can you *do* about these feelings? If you're feeling
especially angry, sit down at your desk and write down every
detail of those feelings. If you're angry because he was taken
from you so young in life, pound out every detail of your rage:
"It's not fair. He was such a good father...he worked so
hard...he never abused his body with unhealthy habits." Now
wad that paper up and throw it down on the floor, stomp on it.
Let those feelings out.

Writing the thank-you notes for food, flowers, memorials,
cards, and other kindnesses can be a curing catharsis. As you
write these notes and force yourself to remember all the good—
but sad-to-remember-right-now—times with your husband,

your mutual friends, and family, you are helping yourself to heal. Cry. As much as it hurts, cry. Failing to take time to cry may result in later problems.

"Why Can't I Cry?"

During one of our "Life Strategies," seminars, Sharon waited until everyone had left, then approached Donnette.

"Why can't I cry?" she asked in a strangled voice. "I'm just overwhelmed with everything. I loved my husband, but I don't think I can even breathe deeply enough to cry."

As Donnette talked to Sharon, it became apparent that in the year after her husband's death, Sharon's children had written all the thank-you notes for food, flowers, and cards. They had arranged for any travel she did and dealt with lawyers, accountants, insurance agents, and financial planners. In every way her children could, they had smoothed out her life so that she wouldn't have to deal with her husband's death. And Sharon, under their well-meaning help, was smothering.

Donnette recommended that Sharon take the steps that would let her work through her grief. It was suggested that she sit down and read all the letters and cards that had been sent after her husband's death. Later on she could dig through the memorabilia of their life together. She had been walled off from her life with her husband as surely as if actual bricks had been mortared around her. She had to break through that wall and revel in the life they had had together before she could grieve for the loss.

Grief is normal. It is the mind and body's way of dealing with loss. Don't let well-meaning loved ones try to seal you up in a safe little compartment where you can't get on with the healing process of grief.

Guilt

How many people do you know who have done everything right, who have never spoken out in anger, who did the absolute maximum to help others? Are you feeling guilt? Do you feel ashamed that you got to live while he was taken? Are you disgusted with yourself for not doing enough for him when he was alive? Is there a part of you that is relieved—and feeling guilty about being relieved?

To cope with guilt, try to make some realistic assessments at a time when you're feeling "up." If you still feel guilt after realistic assessments, think of what you can do now that will make you feel better about what you feel you did—or did not do. Realistically consider the following questions:

- Do you feel guilty because you think you could have spent more time at his side? Remember, you also had your other obligations to your family, your job. If after realistic assessment you still feel guilty, then turn that negative into a positive. Use that feeling to become a compassionate friend who remembers to take food to someone just home from the hospital.

- Did you really fail to tell him how much you loved him when he was alive? If so, then make a point tell your parents, your sisters and brothers, your children, and your friends how much you love them and how much they mean to you. Tell coworkers how much their steady work and support mean to you. Give someone a sincere compliment whenever possible.

- Do you feel guilty that you are alive when he is not? You know deep down that this is not a logical feeling, but you still have it. If you feel you must physically do something about this guilt in order to make it go away, then work in his memory. Make a scrapbook about his life to pass on to a child, grandchild, niece, or nephew. Make a donation in his name to a cause he favored.

- Do you feel guilty that you are feeling relief after his death? Many of us experience this relief, and the guilt that comes with it. Consider rationally if you can: Would he have wanted to live on as an invalid? Would you want him to continue to suffer pain and despair? Begin to remember the healthy, happy times and know that he, too, was happy then. Cherish those thoughts. Turn them into mental videos that you play and replay.

Fear of Imposing

Bess, a thirty-two-year-old mother of three, confided: "My friends keep offering to help—and frankly, I really need all the help I can get right now, but I hate to impose on them. Do they really mean it, or are they just being nice?"

Right after your husband dies, people may offer to cook for you, drive you places, even clean house for you. Here's the nice surprise: They mean it! People who have known you and your husband want to help you.

- If you're feeling reluctant to "impose," please keep telling yourself, "My friends mean it when they say they want to help me." Please don't turn these people away. If possible, let them do the nice things they want to do for you.
- Some people issue a blanket offer: "Let me know if I can do anything—anything at all." These people mean it too. As time goes on, let them know what they can do.
- You'll feel less like you're imposing if you let friends know your needs ahead of time. If you know you will need a ride to the airport, ask a friend a few days in advance if it would be convenient to take you.
- Return the favor when you are able to. Take your friend to the airport next time she needs a ride. If you are often driven places by a friend and cannot return the favor, offer to pay for the gasoline, or buy dinner sometime.
- Say thank you in writing. Write a brief thank-you note after someone has helped you. There's no need to get elaborate; just express your sincere gratitude.

Acceptance

"Some days I feel like I'm going to make it just fine. I can joke and laugh with the kids—look forward to a rafting trip the next weekend. Then a few days later I'm miserable again. Do other people have these sinking spells after they've been doing so well?" asked Bonnie, an accountant who participated in one of our seminars.

Getting over grief is not like getting over a cold. You don't get better each day. You have occasional good days, then bad days, then less bad days; then good days finally outnumber the bad ones.

Then it will not hurt as badly to remember. There will be a day when you can smile when you remember.

Then there will be a day when you begin to contemplate a life on your own.

Is It All Right to Feel Happy Again?

Yes. You don't have to cherish and hold on to your grief forever. Let it go, and enjoy the almost-forgotten feeling of smiling. You know your loved one loved your smile!

DONNETTE: *Say to yourself, "It's okay to feel happy!" I remember feeling that people would look at me funny if I smiled, that they'd be thinking, "What's with the merry widow?" But happiness did come to me. Both Barbara and I started going through the strange feelings of happiness at the same time. All of a sudden we both just felt elation, but we were embarrassed to talk about it. I had a job I loved, and she did too. We were with friends, and some of our problems were being worked out. Things started to look up—maybe it didn't look like it to other people, but from where we'd come, we were doing really well.*

And we had to actually let ourselves enjoy feeling good. We'd felt grief for so long we had to relearn how to do without it.

How Long Do I Wait Before Taking Off My Wedding Ring?

When you are almost ready to stop wearing your wedding ring, go slow. Give yourself time to make the transition.

Try leaving the ring off for a day or so. There may be days when you wish to put it back on. If that's the way you feel that day, by all means, do so. Also, you might try wearing it on your other hand. (You may have to have it sized.)

Donnette had her wedding ring remounted and wears it

frequently on her right hand. There are no hard and fast answers. You must do what feels right to you.

Getting Help for Overwhelming Grief

"It's been almost two years, and I can't seem to get over this overwhelming grief," confided Alice, a young widow with three children whose husband was killed in an auto accident.

If grief threatens to crush you, if it will not leave you alone and has gone on more than a year, get professional help. Contact your local hospice and ask for a counselor. Sit down with your pastor, priest, or rabbi. Call the city or county health department, the local United Way or Family Services and ask for referrals of mental health professionals. Perhaps they will recommend that you attend a support group before you undertake one-on-one counseling.

There is help for you.

YOUR CHILDREN'S GRIEF

"It was two hours before the funeral. The children and I were dressing to leave for the service. I was horrified when I overheard my eighty-one-year-old great-aunt telling my tearful thirteen-year-old son, Lee, 'You're the man of the house now. You must be very brave and not cry.'

"Lee needs to be able to cry, to express his sadness—just like I do," said Margaret, whose husband died of leukemia.

Margaret is so right. But it's hard to be the comfort*er* when you need to be the comfort*ee*, isn't it? Here are some tips for dealing with your children's grief:

Honor their feelings. Margaret was sensitive to Lee's need to express his grief. Your children are probably feeling the same emotions—shock, denial, confusion, fear, anger, depression, and guilt—that you are.

When you hear confusion and anger—such as, "Mom, it's just not fair! Why couldn't it have been someone else's dad?—be honest in your empathy. "No, it doesn't seem fair to me all the time either. But we must remember that nearly everyone who dies has someone who loves and misses them too."

It is healthy for children of all ages to share their guilt feelings: "Mom, sometimes I was so bad—I stayed out late those times and worried Dad so much. I spent too much money last year in college, when I knew things were tough at home. I feel so awful for all those dumb things I did."

When you hear those concerns, be honest and empathetic about guilt feelings, 'Tom, I have felt guilty myself for things I've done and not done. But most of the time you were a fine son, and I was a loving wife. Let's remember that none of us is perfect. And Dad loved us both just as much as we loved him."

Be honest about your own feelings. Confess to your children: "I miss Dad too. I am very, very sad that he is gone, and right now it's hard to think about him without crying. And sometimes I do cry. And you need to cry, too, when you feel like it. Yet I know that there will be a day when we can all remember the good times we had together with Dad and smile."

Be reassuring. This may be your children's first close encounter with the death of a loved one. They may fear that they are going to lose you too. Reassure them that you will be there for them.

They may fear their own death. Answer their questions as honestly as you can, and when you don't feel that you have just the right words, explain that you have a counselor, psychologist, physician, or clergy friend who can better help you answer that question. After discussing your child's questions with your chosen consultant, you might wish to make an appointment and go together for a visit.

Do what seems right about the funeral. Most hospice counselors advise that even young children should be given the opportunity to say good-bye, and should attend the funeral. Some children may want to view the body. Others may be terrified at the very thought. Here, you must do what seems right for the individual child.

Stay aware of your child's need to talk. About four weeks after the funeral, eleven-year-old former angel Amy became quarrelsome, tearful, and belligerent at every turn. She hurled her hairbrush at her sister and her tap-dancing shoes against the wall.

Behavior such as impatience, anger, and breaking into tears without obvious provocation are all normal behavior during the grief process. Often it's a signal of their need to talk out their concerns, fears, and sadness about their loss of their father. Amy's perceptive mother remarked, "It appears you're feeling pretty angry. Are you feeling upset that Dad is gone? Do you want talk about it?"

Look into a support group for your children. Many hospices have bereavement programs, such as "Rainbows" for children, and "Spectrum" for teenagers. Call your local hospice.

Educate yourself about what your children are feeling. Some suggested reading:

- *Why Did Daddy Die? Helping Children Cope With the Loss of a Parent*, by Linda Alderman (Pocket Books, 1991)
- *Learning to Say Good-Bye: When a Parent Dies*, by Eda LeShan (Simon and Schuster, 1976)
- *Teenagers Face to Face With Bereavement*, by Karen Gravelle and Charles Haskins (Silver Burdett, 1989)
- *The Fall of Freddie the Leaf: A Story of Life for All Ages*, by Leo Buscaglia, Ph.D. (Henry Holt, 1982)
- *About Dying: An Open Family Book for Parents and Children Together*, by Sara Bonnett Stein, with photographs by Dick Fran (Walker, 1974)

SURVIVAL TIP

Do not hesitate to seek professional help for dealing with your or your children's grief. Call your local Family Services, United Way, hospice or church for referrals.

PLANNING FOR THE LONG HAUL

During the acceptance stage of the grief process, you will be able to make a plan for the long haul. Now is the time for you to think beyond the present to a future you are more able to control yourself. It is time to make a long-range plan for your life.

Get a strong understanding of your current financial status and decide if it's time to make changes. See chapter 9 for how to choose and work with your advisers—such as attorney, accountant, financial adviser, and insurance agents. See chapters 10, 11, 12, and 13 for business tips and helpful hints about money.

Are you interested in a new career or a new direction for the career you have now? We have included chapters on utilizing your own personal bank account of life experiences to start a new career (chapter 6), setting and accomplishing goals (chapter 7), and strategies for landing a job (chapter 8).

We urge you to get your own estate in order. Bring your will up to date. Consider planning for who might care for you if you are no longer able to do so. A sobering fact is that through advances in modern medicine, increased exercise, and proper nutrition, we are seeing situations where the body outlives the brain. Through a living trust, you can choose the trustee who would look after you and your interests—and make it easier for that person to manage your assets. See chapter 10, "Protecting Your Assets" for advice about wills, trusts, general durable power of attorney, and durable power of attorney for health care.

DONNETTE: *You have learned through your loss, including some information you never imagined you'd need to learn. You have also learned that you are, in the final analysis, responsible for your own life and happiness. Repeatedly, Barbara and I had to remind ourselves: "No one is responsible for me but me. No one is supposed to take care of me but me, and no one is supposed to make me happy but me. And with God's help, I can do it."*

You, too, are surviving and ultimately will triumph over this monumental transition in your life.

PART II

PRACTICAL MATTERS

4

Creating Your Own Support Group

BARBARA: *During all our hard times, before and after divorce and widowhood, Donnette and I presented our best faces to the world, bottling up most things inside us. It was only with our closest friends that we could share the truth, the real truth about how we felt. We cannot imagine how we would have gotten through all our trials without "the Lunch Bunch," our own support group. The Lunch Bunch was a group of our creation, but it can be a source of support for anyone who needs it.*

Five years before Barbara's divorce and Mac's death, we and four friends decided to form a group to meet for lunch once a week with no important purpose in mind. Just a group of kindred souls meeting, enjoying each other's company, talking about whatever we wanted to talk about, and having lunch. For lack of a better name, we dubbed ourselves the "Lunch Bunch." Little did we realize how far this group would go together.

Together we have weathered:

- Two divorces
- The death of one husband
- More problems with children than we can count
- One remarriage

- Lawsuits
- Fear of losing financial security

When we say *we* have been through all of the above, we mean just that. We went through everything together. No one was struggling all alone. We formed a group that is stronger than the sum of the parts, and we feel as if our group is for life.

The first year or so, we just did our melding together. Some of us were really good friends of two or three of the others, but none of us were good friends with everyone. Over the years a closeness grew, but it is important to note that it did not occur overnight. Those of us who found it easier to talk began to open up first. At last, the most private among us began to talk.

Now we are truly all for one and one for all. We can and do tell each other anything and everything we want to, and know that we will not be judged. And we will not be given advice unless we ask for it.

Barbara feels that she has taken the most from the group and given the least. Donnette feels that she has taken the most and given the least. Probably each member of the group feels the same way.

BARBARA: *I remember so well that during my married life I wore a constant smile and "everything's wonderful" demeanor, trying to fool the world around me. I never shared the real truth with anyone. We all put on our best faces, most of the time, bottling up most things inside us. But through our trials, Donnette and I were able to share the truth—the real truth—of how we really, really felt, with each other and with our "Lunch Bunch." But we must work at friendships, close friendships. They do not just occur by accident.*

When life is tossing you about and you feel as though change is the only constant in your life, the single most important thing that you must do is keep a positive attitude. Of course, if that were easy, everybody would do it. Staying positive is pretty hard to do when you are burdened with thoughts of being alone. And "alone" is the key word. Sometimes the hardest thing to do is to reach out to others so that you don't feel all alone. But it's one of the most helpful things you can do.

Too many times, we sit back wondering where our friends are when we need them. If only someone would call...if only somebody would reach out...While maybe, in the house next door, there is a woman wishing someone would call her, hoping somebody will reach out and be a friend....

Most of the people around you are not mind readers (unless by some chance you work for the Psychic Network). It's up to you to find a support group. You're going to have to let someone know you need a friend, and that you're willing to go to some trouble to have one. In fact, you're so willing to work this out, you will put together a whole *group* of friends.

How can you form your own support group or find one that fits you? Well, we wouldn't ask the question if we didn't have an answer.

Consider forming your own tailor-made support group. There are some groups which already exist that you might consider joining, and we will talk more about that in the second part of this chapter. For now, let's talk about creating a support group that suits *you*.

GETTING IT OFF THE GROUND

1. First, make the decision. "Today, I am going to gather together a group of friends who will support me as I will support them." Yes, say it out loud.
2. Make a list of the people you know. Think of them in terms of places—women you know from church, school, your child's school, organizations to which you belong, the office, your neighborhood, exercise class, sports. Don't discriminate, just write down every name you can think of.
3. Now narrow it down. With whom would you enjoy going to lunch? Whom would you like to sit down with over a cup of cappuccino? Whom do you admire? With whom do you feel a

kinship? On the other hand, who is always too busy to stop and say hello? Is there someone on your long list to whom you just can't relate?

4. Suppose you look over the list carefully and find there is only one person you'd really like to get together with. Then call her and propose that between the two of you, you form a support group. Brainstorm. The two of you can probably come up with names of more people together than you can alone. Then if you add a third person, the *three* of you can brainstorm....

How Many to Invite

What's the best size for a support group? Well, twenty is too many and two is too few.

The group should be large enough so that when one or two can't attend, there's still a gathering.

The group should be small enough to sit comfortably around a restaurant or kitchen table, or gather in a living room without sitting shoulder to shoulder.

We recommend six to eight people. That has been the right size for us because even in the busiest of times, there are always at least two or three who can get together to meet. The group is large enough to accommodate different viewpoints, but even with eight people, it is possible for each person to have a chance to speak.

Whom to Invite

Now, remember, we said you have to work at not being alone. Don't grab the first eight people you see. You need to be with people who can share your joys and sorrows, who want to commit time and effort to an important cause, who can give and take, listen and share.

Of course it's not easy to find six or eight people who meet those criteria. But it's not impossible. Ask people you would like to spend some time with. Remember, this is a long-term goal, not a temporary idea to help you through a crisis.

Your new best friends don't have to be just like you. In fact, you could try for diversity. Whatever makes you comfortable. They don't all have to be the same age, or the same race, divorced or widowed, young mothers or grandmothers.

The most important point is to pick people you feel are basically honest, who treat you with respect and seem glad to see you. Remember, the key word in support group is *support*.

Where to Meet

Our Lunch Bunch meets at a different restaurant each week. We like having variety, but members of other support groups swear by meeting in the same place every time. It might be best to start by gathering in the same place until getting together becomes a habit, then add variety to see how the group responds to it.

For us, it's been fine to vary the location but not to change the time and day. We met for years on Monday at noon. Then one of the women asked if we could change it to Thursdays because she wanted to meet with a weight-control group on Mondays. We made the switch and almost immediately regretted it. For some reason, it was just too hard to meet on Thursday.

After about a year of having conflicts on meeting days and feeling as though she was becoming less and less of a member, Barbara said, "I'm missing the most meetings, and I feel I need all of you the most. Could we go back to Mondays?"

You'd have been amazed at how relieved everyone was. Nobody wanted to say anything, but they felt just like Barbara did. Fortunately, our dieter had quit her Monday weigh-ins and could make the switch with us.

The lesson we learned was that it is important not to change what is working well for the largest number of the group. We would have to think long and hard before we would ever change again.

Here are some places to consider:

- Restaurants. Where can you get a table that seats six to eight people? Can you hear over the din of food service? Is the food good and is there variety to handle differing tastes? Is there a little privacy? How are the prices? (Every member pays her own way.)

- Churches. Use a parlor or fellowship room—nothing too big or formal. Some churches have nurseries and child-care workers who will watch your children at little or no cost while you meet. For some women with young children, a little time away from the children may be the best part of the meeting!
- Homes. This is an obvious choice. But can you honestly say having the meeting at your house won't make you run around cleaning before everyone comes over? Do you need that pressure?
- Public buildings. Look for free rooms with coffeemakers, comfortable chairs, and lighting that doesn't make everyone look as though they work the night shift at the police station.
- Offices. Don't mix business with your personal life. But if you have no other place to meet and someone has an office with a comfortable conference room you may use in the evenings or on weekends, it might be suitable. It's really a last resort, though.

When to Meet

- Lunch. Good for working women, mixed groups. Almost everyone takes a break in the middle of the day to eat lunch.
- Late mornings or afternoons. When the children are taking a nap or are in day care.
- Evenings. Evening meetings must have a definite ending time so that they don't drag on too long. After-dinner meetings may best fit your group's schedules. Dinner meetings at a restaurant are an alternative for women who are alone in the evenings. It's a good way to fight that lonely feeling that comes with cooking for one.

We meet once a week. We don't have much catching up to do if there are only seven days between each lunch. With a month in between meetings, the small things you've thought about often seem too insignificant to mention. Our Lunch Bunch gets together with the same fervor some people devote to going to the gym. It's as good for the soul as the gym is for the body.

If getting together once a week seems too frequent, try every two weeks, or even once a month. You'll find a schedule that fits.

MAKING IT WORK

Pick a day and time and stick to it. Being consistent will make it easier to remember. But most importantly, make your support group a priority. Vow that only the most dire emergency will sway you from joining your friends at the appointed time. Make sure the members of your group understand you are asking them to make that commitment too.

Don't expect to feel the same closeness to every member of the group. Over the years, we have been closer to different people in the group depending on situations and needs, which have been different at different times. You're creating a "family" here, and just like any family, you're more connected and more able to talk to some relatives than others.

What are the hallmarks of a good support group?

First, the members come to each other's aid in times of need, not because it is expected but because they really care. Does that happen overnight? Of course not.

When Donnette's husband, Mac, died, the Lunch Bunch had been together for five years. We were so close that all the group wanted to do was try to take away some of Donnette's pain. We cooked food for her, drove her places, helped clean her house, answered the phone, and cried with her. In short, we each did what we knew Donnette would do for us if we were in her place. When one of us is hurting, the rest "circle the wagons."

Second, blame is not the game. Instead of sitting around complaining and blaming people who failed us, we try to keep things on the positive side. After a long story that makes us all groan and think that some "foe" should be on the first shuttle to Mars, someone might say, "Yes, she's a cad, she's a rat—but you're the person who's important here. How are you doing?"

That doesn't mean nobody can complain, but our reason for being together is to be better, not angrier.

The group provides support "after hours." The strong bond between members exists not only when we are having lunch together. For example, we all know that after a divorce, some people may take sides. Either they're his friends or they're hers. Because Barbara had a strong support group, she was fortunate enough that her friends who were couples continued to include her as they had when she was married.

With a group to sustain you, you feel a sense of control over your life, a commitment to your work, interests, and relationships, and an ability to see stress as a challenge rather than a threat.

In the group, you should have:

• Freedom to think without being ashamed
• Freedom to talk
• Freedom to connect with others

How can you create a group which lets each member achieve these freedoms?

Rules of the House

In one of your first sessions, let the group establish some ground rules. Such rules could include:

• First and foremost, be kind to one another. There are plenty of other places where you will encounter put-downs, criticism, sarcasm, and lack of consideration. This is, by definition, a *support* group.
• Confidences must stay in the group. No matter how fascinating the gory details are, don't go blabbing them all over town. Not to your spouse, not to people you think will never even know the members of your group.
• Try not to interrupt each other.
• Don't gossip about group members who are not present. It will make others wonder what you say about them when they're not there.

- Rejoice in each other's triumphs. Each of you is made better when one succeeds.
- All group members are important and therefore should make an effort to come to the meetings, whenever humanly possible.

Once the group has brainstormed and come up with rules, you may want to write them down and seal your good intentions.

The Roles People Play

Each person brings something unique and special to the group. The diversity of personalities will create an environment where you can share, support each other, and grow in positive change.

In time, the members of your group will probably prove themselves to fall into certain types, just like our Lunch Bunch. Some of these roles may be played by several people, and some people may play several roles. We have:

The cheerleader, who encourages us to succeed and emotionally nurtures us in times of trouble.

The esteem builder, who helps us have a strong self-image by assuring us we can succeed at anything we wish.

A constructive critic, who plays the devil's advocate, just to help us come up with new ideas. Many times we need people to poke holes in our ideas to get us to come up with new thoughts.

The leveler, who brings us back to earth when we are not thinking straight.

The catalyst, who provides the spark to get us moving on a project or long-term goal. Catalysts are enthusiastic about you and your work, so therefore they energize you.

The role model is someone you want to imitate. She may have a sunny disposition you wish you had, so you will try to be more like her.

The organizer helps in your day-to-day activities, saving you time and helping you be efficient.

The role of adviser is played by everyone. It's so much easier to see how to improve everyone else's life but your own! When we bring our problems to the group we are often seeking advice, but we can also tell everyone we don't want advice and they have to refrain from giving it. The members of our group have become so close that we are able to accept advice without feeling that it's criticism, and we're pretty good at giving advice gently and nonjudgmentally.

Personal Ground Rules

Besides thinking about rules for the group as a whole, it is important that you think of what kind of role you want to play in order to be a "giving" member of the group. Here are some good rules to live by:

- Do not bleed the group dry by always being the "taker." A support group is just like any other relationship. Take requires give. Listen to the others as much as you talk. This is especially hard to do when you are hurting.
- Honesty is, as it has always been, the best policy. You are establishing a safe place where each of you tells the truth about how you feel and how your world is going. You might have to be the first to admit that you sublimated your sorrow in an entire carton of Rocky Road ice cream. I'll bet you'll find you're not alone.
- Because your friends care about you, they may try to find answers to all your problems. You do not have to take any of their advice. It's okay to preface any story with the words, "Now, I'm not really looking for a solution for this, I just want to get it out."
- Because you care about your friends, listen to their suggestions. You do not have to follow their advice, but you should give it respectful consideration.
- Do not feel embarrassed about feeling weak and needing the support of the others. It's normal.
- No matter how busy you are, it is important to get with your group. That hour can restore your soul.
- Realize that not everyone will be able to open up. One of our group feels uncomfortable displaying emotion, and it is difficult for her to let the rest know she needs support. She does

not know how to ask. We have finally become able to recognize when she needs help.

- Don't pass judgment. The woman who has opened up to you deserves your support, just because she has been honest enough to say how she feels.
- Don't be quick to criticize other people's families. Emotions may run high and one of the group may disparage everything about her own husband, her mother-in-law, her unemployed son. Tomorrow she may be over her anger and resent the rotten things you chimed in and said about them.

The Format

In the long run, your group will evolve to a comfortable format. In the early days, it may need a little prodding.

Our gang has been together so long that the group attention instinctively shifts to the person who most needs it. We don't think about where we sit or attempt to impose any topics of discussion. The years together have enabled us to dispense with any formality.

At first, however, a little order helps. Here are a few things you might try to get the group moving.

- Try to sit by a different person every time. Get to know everyone.
- Allow time for each person to say a little something about herself each time. Out loud. To the group. Otherwise, unless you're sitting next to a person, you might never know what is happening in her life.
- You may consider having a leader to get things going. That position could change every week, or every month, or every six months. You could do away with a leadership position if you decide you don't need it.
- Talk about issues that affect us all. Bring newspaper clippings about stress, child care, medical research.
- Talk about the common as well as the lofty. Have you found a great recipe that takes five minutes to fix and tastes like a million bucks? Or maybe you have seen a funny cartoon. Bring copies for everyone.

- Make one session a "genealogy" lunch. Have everyone bring photos of their parents, sisters, and brothers. Each person can talk briefly about her childhood.
- Really *listen* when someone needs to talk. That's probably the key to the group's success.
- If there is one person in your group who talks too much and dominates every conversation, consider putting a time limit on monologues.
- A topic of discussion could be introduced in each gathering, if talk doesn't seem to be forthcoming. The danger here, of course, is that discussions of this kind aren't really conducive to personal exchange. You might solve the plight of the world and still never talk about the emptiness of your home now that your children are gone.

Remember, many times you cannot tote all of your burdens alone, and there is such immense strength in having your group. A small group gives us energy to stay committed to our purpose. It gives us strength because we each think, "If that person can do it, I can do it." It gives us strength and energy to keep going and provides accountability for our actions.

When you have the capacity to confide and share your raw and often painful feelings, it takes some of the load off your shoulders and provides support, stress relief, and new ideas for solving your problems. Don't let your group become so formal that you can't talk to each other.

TAKING THE GROUP TO NEW HEIGHTS

When one of our group decided her marriage was over after several years of counseling, to no avail, we were all there. The week her husband was to move out, we were having lunch and somebody said, "We should get out of town," and someone else chimed in, and before we knew it, we were all packed and on our way to Ruidoso, New Mexico, for a weekend in the mountains.

We were all feeling pretty righteous, sure that we had done a fine thing for our friend, getting her out of town. It wasn't until we were far away from home that we began to realize she wasn't the only one helped by the trip.

We slept late, didn't get out of our robes until lunchtime. We relaxed, laughed, ate, drank thick hot coffee. And we talked. Who would have known that we had so much talk in us? We resolved issues we didn't even imagine we had. We unwound. We got even closer to each other. On the way home, our friend thanked us. Then each and every one of us thanked her—for helping us break away from our daily routines and form a closer group.

A Lunch Bunch isn't just for lunch. It's for morning, evening, divorce, widowhood, fun, and sorrow. It's for you, and it's for me. It's for life, and for making life better.

JOINING AN EXISTING GROUP

If you would love to be a part of a support group but you can't put one together yourself, find one that is already established that meets your needs.

Find out what is available by looking in your newspaper or on a college bulletin board, or calling the chamber of commerce, organizations such as the YMCA, your church, affiliates of national groups, or the offices of Human Resources, Human Development, or Mental Health. Then visit the groups that interest you. Don't be afraid to go once and never return or to visit several times if you cannot decide if the group is right for you.

Some of these groups might charge a membership fee. If you feel the credentials of the organization are top-notch and the reputation is good—and you can afford it—then the cost is worth it. Ask around. Talk to someone who attends or used to be a part of the support group. It may be very helpful to have a qualified, certified group leader who sets the agenda and helps set the direction discussions take.

It's worth finding the right group. It might make all the difference in the world to you, as it did for us.

5

Teaching Others How to Treat You

DONNETTE: *Two months after Mac died, I decided to go to the video shop to rent a movie. After wandering around for about thirty minutes, I was back in my car, empty-handed, with tears streaming down my face. And do you know why? Because I did not know which movie to rent. I honestly did not know what kind of movie I myself preferred. We had always gotten the kind of movie he wanted, gone to the kind of restaurant he wanted. And I didn't resent that. I didn't even think about it. I never thought about it back then. It was my way of life and I was happy doing whatever he wanted.*

I did not realize that in some ways I was not challenging myself to develop my own tastes and opinions. It now makes me sad to hear someone say, "I have tried for so long to be what everyone wants me to be that I have no idea who I really am." I know how they feel. I know how you feel if you feel that way. But it is possible—and a great deal of fun—to grow up and learn, at the ripe old age of fifty-four—what I really think and what I really like!

BARBARA: *We teach people how to treat us. We teach our husbands and families what we will accept and what we think we are worth. Then... it is very easy to blame others for what happens to us. "This would not have happened if he had not done so-and-so.... If it had not been for him, I would have done thus-and-so; he held me back." Not true. Life is made up of choices. We choose the one we marry, we choose our friends, and we choose the way we are treated by those persons. They do not treat us any way but the way we allow them to.*

WHOLE, NOT HALF

For a long time, it was the two of you. You were a couple, a pair, linked in everyone's minds. Now you are alone. You feel like half of a whole, far less than just two minus one. That may be how you feel right now, but that's not how you really are.

Everything that made you lovable in the first place is still there. Your personality, your tastes, your quirks, your style of embracing life. You are not less than you were. You are one whole, wonderful person. You may hurt, you may cry, you may be lonely. But you are not *half* a person. You are *all* you.

You may feel as though you must rush to fill the void. You might charge out to parties, run after a man, dash after a new career. We're here to give you permission to take your time. Now, precisely because you are alone, you can make careful decisions about your life. You don't need to apologize for being alone. You can be pretty darned good company, all by yourself.

If you married young, you probably went from being your daddy's little girl to being a wife. Now, for the first time, you're nobody's baby.

But, darn it, you're still treated like one. Your friends give you advice. Your parents worry about you. Your office mates are doing part of your job along with theirs. Why won't they treat you like an adult?

Are you actually ready to be treated like an adult? What have you done lately to instill in your family and friends the faith that you can make it alone? First off, thank your lucky stars that there are people who care enough about you to want to help. Then set about taking the burden off them.

Drive your car to the Quicky Lube and have the oil changed, all by yourself. Don't wait until your dad calls to ask if you've had it done. While you're there, check to see when your inspection sticker expires. Write the expiration date down on your calendar so you will have another opportunity to prove your competence to yourself.

Get to the office earlier than anyone else and spend some time organizing your desk before the phones start ringing. Make a list of things you need to do. Do *not* spend your workday answering personal phone calls. There is nothing more upsetting to your coworkers than seeing you crying (or cursing!) on the phone. Do that after work, on your own time.

Make yourself balance your checkbook. A major step in teaching others how to treat you is knowing where you stand— and knowing that you can stand on your own two feet.

After your income tax statement has been prepared, do you look over it carefully before you sign it? Many times, because an accountant has prepared it, we sign it and think we will read it later...but later never comes! This tax return is your responsibility, and you need to read it and ask questions. If there is something that you do not understand, ask your accountant to explain it to you (and in language you can understand!). Accountants are human and they can make mistakes. Remember, if you are audited, "the buck stops with you," not the accountant.

Get very familiar with your investments. Many married women tend to let their husbands handle the investments, and perhaps you were among them, as we were. But now you are alone! You are responsible for the investments, and you must understand every aspect of your portfolio. We have a good friend who was divorced. Sharon made a great deal of money during the oil boom of the early eighties. She started an investment club so that she would know and understand how to invest that money wisely. Now she is remarried to a former banker. She was so successful with her investments before they married, he insisted that she continue to handle her investments and his too!

We may feel inadequate when we first start to be responsible for ourselves, but *we can learn*—we can read—*Money* magazine is an excellent resource. Take an investment class at a college. *You want to take care of yourself and you need to take care of yourself.* You cannot imagine the great sense of satisfaction you will have!

PROTECTING YOURSELF AS A CONSUMER

According to *Why Women Pay More: How to Avoid Marketplace Perils*, by Frances Cerra Whittelsey (Center for Study for Responsive Law, 1991), a study on price discrimination showed that 42 percent of the used car dealers surveyed stuck women with higher prices than they asked from men. How can you avoid such universal discrimination?

Follow the old Boy Scout motto, "Be prepared." Do your homework before you shop. When you are looking for a car, buy a copy of *Consumer's Guide*. Go to several car lots and drive the cars. Make yourself compare prices, even when it seems like too much trouble. If a salesperson treats you like an idiot, walk off the lot. If that lot has the car you want, come back later and deal with a different salesperson.

If you are upset about any product or service, you can do two things. Go somewhere else or complain. If you choose to complain, use these techniques:

- Round up all relevant information, including sales receipt, product box, date you wrote the check, and the department or location where you made the purchase.
- Start with your local store and work up. The department manager may be able to help you. If not, try the store manager. Then go on to the chain office, if there is one. Let each higher office know you want to work with them to right the situation.
- Keep a record of each person you talk to, when you made the call, what was said.
- If an oral complaint doesn't help, put it in writing. Call the store and find out the name of the local manager, or the regional manager, or, heck, the owner of the whole darned

company. Furnish as many facts, names, and dates as possible. Include your name, phone number, and address on any correspondence so that you can be contacted.

- Send copies, not originals, of any documents.
- Know your rights as a consumer. According to Ralph Charell, author of *Satisfaction Guaranteed* (Linden Press, 1985), you can call the state or federal agency that handles your type of complaint and ask to speak directly to their on-staff counsel. The attorney can provide copies of laws that directly outline your rights and can even give you a list of people who will receive copies of all correspondence about this complaint.
- Look at your local library for the *Consumer's Resource Handbook* for addresses of consumer representatives and federal and state agencies that handle consumer complaints, or write: Consumer Information Center, Dept. 59ZZ, Pueblo, CO 81009.
- Find the 800 phone numbers of many businesses in AT&T's directory of toll-free numbers. A copy costs $14.99 and is available by calling 1-800-426-8686.
- Sandwich your complaint between two compliments. For example, "I have had excellent treatment for the three years I have been shopping at Pricely Pharmacy. I was disappointed that the sales clerk working in perfumes at two P.M. on Wednesday, April 21, was rude and unwilling to help. That is so unlike the excellent service I've come to expect here."
- Try not to lose your temper. You are in the right and you just have to be persistent. Think of this as a test of your diligence.

PROTECTING YOURSELF FROM MEDICAL PROFESSIONALS

If you have recently been widowed or divorced, don't underestimate the effect that has on your entire body. Before you rush to a doctor, you might consider treating yourself to some tender loving care. (You certainly deserve it.) Get some good vitamins, add some exercise to your day, make sure you are eating decently. (See chapter 1, "Feeling Better Right This Minute.")

This does not mean, however, that you should accept the

belittling opinion that your illness is all in your head and you should just be a good girl and get over it. Get over any doctor who tells you that!

And speaking of doctors, another area where you may be a pushover is in the medical profession. Do not let a doctor rush you into anything before you have a chance to consider your options. Remember that you are always entitled to a second opinion, as well as your own choice of treatment.

If you are diagnosed with an illness, find out everything you can about it. Go to the local library and get all the books that focus on that condition. Call the Help Lines listed in those books or surf the Internet, if you want to know more.

Yes, you can mention new treatments to your doctor. Ask questions. Write down everything the doctor says. Be sure you tell him or her about all your symptoms, since some of them may contradict others.

Here are some techniques for dealing with your doctor from Dr. Peter H. Berczeller, who published an article in the June 15, 1994, issue of *Bottom Line Personal* magazine titled "How to Deal With Your Doctor More Effectively":

- Don't address your doctor by his or her first name. Keep the relationship professional.
- If your doctor calls you by your first name and you object to that, speak up! Your doctor works for you.
- If your doctor seems uncaring, remember, his or her emotions are kept in check. Don't take it personally. If, however, you cannot get answers to questions you want or you feel you are not being taken seriously, speak up.
- To get a second opinion, you may ask your doctor to recommend another doctor, or you may seek one out yourself. Most physicians nowadays almost expect this.
- If you are embarrassed to talk to your doctor, remember he or she has studied these subjects for years. It's a good bet that you're not the first nor will you be the last with this condition.
- To keep your family members from interfering with your

treatment, be frank with them about what you want and expect. Don't let someone else take over your relationship with your doctor unless you are really sure that's what you want.

SPEAK UP!

Angie, a woman in one of our workshops, was always furious at her husband. He always forgot her birthday, he never remembered their anniversary. She could have spent all day cooking a wonderful dinner, and he ate it without even noticing how it tasted. Some days she was so aggravated at him she could just scream.

One the other hand, Linda, another participant, talked about her husband, Bruce, who was an absolute dream. For Valentine's Day, Bruce got her the chocolate truffles she loved. For Christmas he gave her the double CD *Evita* soundtrack she has been playing every day since. When she's gone to extra trouble doing something for him, he never fails to acknowledge it, and when she wears a new dress, he stops and looks it over before he kisses her and tells her how great she looks.

What's the difference? Linda tells her husband what she wants, and Angie is still waiting for her husband to guess.

"I figure if I want Bruce to remember my birthday, I can tell him when it is," Linda laughs. "I start in early February mentioning that it's coming on the 27th. When he asks me what I want, I tell him. I don't think anybody really wants to disappoint us, but we're all fallible human beings. We forget, we misread cues. Why should we expect people to be perfect? Bruce wants to please me, and I help him find the way."

When there's something she wants her husband to notice, Linda mentions it.

"Why would anybody keep it a secret if she's gone to a lot of trouble to prepare a special meal? I am honest about it. I might say, 'There were 150 steps to making that vegetable lasagna. Do you like it?' Of course, then he pays attention to what he's eating and says something about it."

She doesn't always get rave reviews for her cooking: "My favorite was when I made a truly awful spaghetti dish and Bruce said, 'You know, this is so darned interesting I want to save it and enjoy it later!' We laughed a lot about that."

She adds, "The other day, Bruce said, 'I don't think I got enough notice for all the work I did cleaning off the porch.' So I told him he did a great job and I was so pleased he'd gone to all that trouble. It may seem set up or funny to ask for praise, but we all need to be reinforced for the good things we do."

How can you apply this advice to your life? Speak up and tell people what you want. Tell your boss you want your name on the project you are working on. Tell your children you'd like them to prepare supper Sunday night. Remind a friend that you have tickets to the theater for the two of you, and mention the date several times so it won't be forgotten. Don't accept a burger with onions and mustard when you asked for ketchup and pickles.

Dial-a-Friend

One of the most frequent things we hear from women who have recently been widowed or divorced is that their friends stay away because they don't know what to say or do. If your life is in upheaval, your friends and acquaintances want to know how to help you, but sometimes they don't know how.

Tell them. Don't feel you have to wait for your friends to make the first move. You can call, you can ask for help, or even extend an invitation to join you for a cup of tea. If you've made an appointment with a friend but you just don't feel like going, tell the honest truth. If you've got to get out of the house or go crazy, call a friend and say, "I know this is short notice, but can you go to a movie *right now?*"

Your friends don't know if they should mention your husband or not. They don't know if you want to cry in front of them, or if you want to keep everything inside. They will take their cues from you, if you let them.

AT WORK

Is it possible to go to work and pretend nothing has happened to you? Probably not. Your boss and coworkers may treat you as if you are a time bomb, about to explode. Here are a few tips that may help you.

- Make lists. You are more prone to forget when your emotions are stirred up, so write down everything you have to do, and check off what you've done.
- Run errands and field personal calls at lunchtime or after work hours. Do not spread these things over your workday. Don't kid yourself, everyone notices.
- Don't enmesh your coworkers in arguments with your ex-husband. Do not allow your ex or anyone else to force you into arguing on your office phone during work hours.
- Eat lunch, even if you have to bring something from home.
- Watch your caffeine intake. If you're drinking caffeinated drinks all day, it will make it even harder to sleep at night, so you'll be even more tired. It's a cycle that's hard to break.
- Is it possible to reschedule new major work projects for a while? You don't want to appear incapable, but if possible, get a postponement for new undertakings.
- Don't feel obligated to take your boss and coworkers into your confidence. All they need to know is broad, general information. Offices can be gossip central—tell too much and it may travel like wildfire.
- Show the people you work with how to treat you. You have had something terrible happen to you, but you are still the same person you have always been. You may need time to recover, but *you will recover.*

BARBARA: *So much of our growing has been as a result of these experiences that were so difficult to come through. After I separated from my husband, so many of my friends asked me if I didn't feel like I had wasted twenty-seven years. Good heavenly days, no. I have two wonderful daughters.... I had a good time. ... I did not do one thing that I did not choose to do. But... I've learned so much during this journey, and... I would never, ever, go back to being the type [of] woman that I was before.*

6

Your Personal Bank Account
of Life Experiences

"I HAVE ALL THE RESOURCES I NEED
TO SURVIVE ON MY OWN"

BARBARA: *A friend once told me soon after I was separated from my husband, "Barbara, because you were married, there was an illusion that you were being taken care of...* but it was only an illusion. *You have always taken care of yourself."* And once I stopped and thought about it, I realized how true that was.

Now, don't let me mislead you. I don't mean that I was going to an office and bringing home a paycheck...what I mean was that because I had spent a great deal of my married life alone, I was the one who made the major decisions about raising the children, emergency decisions in the home, and the day-to-day decisions of taking care of our family. So why should I be frightened? My life was continuing on as it had before. I was taking care of myself just like always and everything was going to be all right. If I had been taking care of myself for the past twenty-seven years, and done all right, I could certainly do it for the next twenty-seven and probably do better, because I had experience! *When I began to assess my life, I realized I have all the resources I need. And you have too.*

To begin to discover your own personal bank account of life experiences, say this aloud: "I have all the resources I need to survive on my own. I *can* take care of myself."

How did that feel? Scary? Overwhelming? We would like to help you see your responsibility for yourself as a positive rather than a negative. Within you is the potential to take care of yourself emotionally and financially, by tapping into your personal bank account of life experiences. What is in it? More than you know.

How Need Creates Discovery

When the Texas economy nose-dived and real estate prices plummeted in the mid-eighties, fifty-two-year-old Judy and her husband Bill were commercial real estate brokers. They had to find a second source of income and find it in a hurry, at a time when most companies were laying people off.

Judy's favorite volunteer work had been in marketing and resale of previously owned merchandise, so she put an ad in the paper saying that she would come by on the last day of a garage or estate sale, pick up the leftovers, and sell them in a very small shop she rented. Then she would share the income on a 50-50 consignment basis with the owners. It was a good idea that combined her personal abilities with a market need.

Judy has moved her consignment shop three different times, each time more than doubling her space. She recently opened a second shop, handling only designer clothes, and a third shop for high-quality furniture. Judy's latest idea is to put consignment resale stores into border towns in Mexico.

What started as an emergency second income has now become a lucrative career. "The need created the discovery," declared Judy.

Dispensing With Self-Doubt

Donnette saw Frances across the room and hurried over to congratulate her. Frances had organized the biggest party at their class reunion, and had done such a fantastic job that everyone was talking about it.

"Frances, this is great! The food is wonderful, the decorations are beautiful, and that photo display you did has really helped us figure out who's who and how we've all changed," Donnette said.

"Oh, well..." Frances replied. "But you, you're the one who's great. Working like you do, giving seminars...I really haven't done anything since high school except keep house and raise children. That's why they made me chairman of the party. That's about all I'm good for."

Frances has raised eight children, taking care of everything from school lunches to a washing machine that runs almost around the clock. For years she has been the unpaid bookkeeper for the family income and outgo. She keeps a calendar on which she lists dates for everything from when to change the filters on the air conditioner to when each child needs to have a checkup. In the middle of everything she does on a daily basis, she took the time to create name tags with our high school pictures on them, coordinate a food committee of ten women, hire a band, and dig out the lyrics to our senior song.

A woman with the same skills as Frances took her life experience and turned it into a smashing success. Donna Olday created Classy Maids, a company that revolutionized house-cleaning by treating it like any other business. When her teams of cleaning people sweep into a home, they powerhouse their way through it, doing in a short time what it would take one person all day to do. Donna Olday based her cleaning business on the experience she had had raising children and keeping her own house clean.

When we hear someone like Frances belittle her own life, we want to tell her, "Stop it right now!" When someone points out your talents and abilities, put away your self-doubt and false modesty.

You have talents and abilities you have acquired from just living life.

Recognizing Your Potential

Start recognizing your potential. We received Karen Bonner's letter a few months after she attended one of our seminars.

I have just finished my first month as Director of Development for the YWCA of Corpus Christi and wanted to thank you for showing me that I had the skills necessary to be a fund-raising consultant and development director. Through your guidance I have been able to turn my teaching skills, organizational skills and selling skills into a lucrative profession. I wanted to stretch myself and do something more interesting with my life but had no confidence that I had the ability to do anything more than continue in our family business where my husband was the responsible party. Little did I know that two years later, he would find it necessary to sell our printing and office supply business and begin a new career himself. With two children in college and one in high school, we knew I would have to help also. Thank you for reminding me that I am the only one responsible for my own financial, emotional, and physical well-being and thank you for helping me recognize my own potential.

Karen discovered her own resources. She discovered talents and abilities that she had acquired from just living life, and *you can too.*

With this in mind, get ready. With this chapter, we are going to help you open up a whole new, exciting world.

Never Too Old

A woman wrote to Dear Abby and said she wanted to go back to college and get her degree, but she would be forty years old in four years when she graduated. Abby's answer was concise: "Well, what age will you be in four years if you do not graduate?"

To every woman who has ever said, "Do I dare, at my age, embark on a new career?" we would like to shout a resounding "Yes!"

Whatever your age is, now is the time to do what you want to do. On a recent vacation in London, a general practitioner told her fellow tourists that she had gone back to school at age forty-nine to get a degree to become a physician. She added, "I love being a doctor, but I think when I retire I will get an archeology degree. Now, that is something I would *really* like to do."

Daring to Dream Big

Ask yourself, "What do I really want to do?"

Think back to the dreams you had when you were a child, your fondest hopes. What would you do if you could do anything, anything at all?

Dare to dream, and while you are at it, dare to dream big. What you can imagine, you can achieve.

Let your mind sift through your dreams for a while. Think about the height of your ambition—and imagine yourself there. Is it possible for you to achieve that? Not if you cannot dream it.

Danielle was working at a big law firm, just as her father, the Harvard law school professor, had wanted. She was one of three children who were all attorneys. She had a six-figure income and was considered one of the brightest and best, probably destined for politics. But one day she woke up and said to herself, "I am just not happy." Danielle decided to do what she had wanted all her life. She went back to school and became a minister. It was something she never thought would be possible, but she had the faith to dream big.

When Danielle was growing up, women were not ministers. They might *marry* ministers, or become church music directors, but the pastorate was not open to them. There are many women who broke down barriers so that Danielle could have the chance to achieve her life's dream. Now she is an example to little girls in her church that the doors to the ministry are not closed to them. Because she dreamed big, she is making it possible for others to do the same—while she is doing what she most wanted to do.

BARBARA DISCOVERS HER DREAM CAREER

Divorce and widowhood, more than anything else, will make you reassess your life. You may be hassled and harried, distraught, angry, or afraid—but more than anything else, you are probably asking yourself what you are going to do with the rest of your life. I know, I did the same.

Not long after my divorce, I was the finance director for the campaign of a friend who was a Texas Supreme Court justice.

The election was set for November, so after that my job would end. I wondered if political fund-raising was what I should continue to do or if there was something else more stable.

Chip, one of my young sons-in-law, sat down with me to work out what I wanted to do; to help me decide what I wanted to be when I "grew up."

The method he used was simple, but so effective it changed my life. I would like to share it with you, because I know if you are searching, it will help you.

First, Chip took a piece of paper, drew a line down the middle, and said, "We'll call the left side 'Real World' and the right side 'Dream.'

I nodded. So far, this was painless.

"Now," Chip said, "On the Real World side, we'll list the things you *could* do to make money. Things you like to do and *could* be happy doing, but not necessarily things you *want* to do for the rest of your life."

Well, we talked, he questioned, I thought.

My degree was in elementary education, but that was not what I would *choose* to do at age fifty-one. But, I said, I did like to teach, because I had enjoyed teaching my fund-raising chairpersons in each town how to do special events.

On the Real World side of the paper, Chip wrote "teacher."

I said I had loved being president of different volunteer organizations. I like looking at the big picture and solving problems and organizing people for action.

Chip wrote "organizer."

I told Chip that I liked fund-raising. I felt very fortunate to have gained the skills I had from all my years as a volunteer, which had made it possible for me to have an exciting career as a fund-raiser. I enjoyed political fund-raising, but it was stressful and I did not want to do it for the rest of my life.

Chip wrote "fund-raiser."

I said I liked to motivate people. I had to keep all my events chairpersons motivated so the fund-raisers they were working on would be successful. I liked getting people excited about what they were doing.

Chip wrote "motivator."

"Anything else?" he asked.

I laughed, "If there is anything else I can do, I surely do not know about it!"

The page that contained my future looked like this:

SKILLS WORKSHEET A

REAL WORLD (Skills I have now)	DREAM (New career/lifestyle)
teacher *organizer* *fund-raiser* *motivator*	

Next, Chip said, "Now for the fun part. The right side of the paper is the Dream side. In your wildest dreams, Barb, what do you wish you could do with the rest of your life?"

I said I had attended a stress seminar about a year earlier and had found myself wanting to motivate people the way the speaker had motivated us. He had taught us to face our stress and find solutions.

"What do you want to motivate and teach people about?" Chip asked.

My answer had two parts:

1. "I wish I could motivate people to take the knowledge and skills they have acquired over the years and turn those skills into a job for pay, like I had done with my fund-raising.
2. "I'd like to motivate people to recognize that every person has a wealth of knowledge on deposit, just waiting to be used."

On the righthand side of the page, under "Dreams," Chip wrote:
"Motivational seminars."

SKILLS WORKSHEET B

REAL WORLD   DREAM
(Skills I have now)   (New career/lifestyle)

teacher *organizer* *fund-raiser* *motivator*	*motivational seminars*

Then Chip said, "We know you have to continue to be a fund-raiser now. But if you develop a seminar where you would be motivating, organizing, and teaching while you continue fund-raising, how long do you think it will be before you can give up fund-raising and do nothing but seminars?"

I was so excited at the prospect that I wanted to say I would start giving seminars right away! But after doing a quick mental calculation, I told him it would probably take about five years.

Chip said, "All right, then go for it."

Under "Steps to Find My Dream," I listed the practical work I had to do to make the transition from the skills I had in the "Real World" to the "Dream" I had of a new career as a motivator. I needed to:

• Begin research to develop a seminar.
• Learn to use a computer.
• Brush up on public-speaking skills.
• Contact other seminar presenters for marketing concepts.

SKILLS WORKSHEET C

REAL WORLD (Skills I have now)	DREAM (New career/lifework)
teacher *organizer* *fund-raiser* *motivator*	*motivational* *seminars*

Steps to Find My Dream (Skills to attain or obstacles to overcome)

1. *Begin research to develop a seminar.*
2. *Learn to use a computer.*
3. *Brush up on public-speaking skills.*
4. *Contact other seminar presenters for marketing concepts*

At the same time I was formulating this dream, Donnette was working in economic development and giving speeches, motivating the community to diversify Midland's economy and attract new residents to the area. She loved motivating people. She dreamed of motivational seminars.

Need I say more? Not five years later but just one short year later, Donnette and I gave our first seminar.

Now it is your turn to find your dream career. So get ready. It is time for you to make your own personal inventory of life experiences and start to make your dreams come true.

YOU DISCOVER YOUR DREAM CAREER

What is in your personal bank account of life experiences? Probably much more than you realize. Let's work on the Skills Worksheet together.

Why not ask a friend or relative to sit down with you and ask you questions to help you start thinking about your talents and abilities? He or she will be able to remind you of talents you may not even be aware you have.

Assessing Your Skills and Talents

We will work on the Real World Side of the Worksheet first (see Worksheet D, on page 98).

Write down all the skills in your personal bank account of life experiences on the "Real World" side of the worksheet. Remember, your "banked experiences" are all the skills you have attained just by living life. You could have a long list on your reality side or just four or five, as I did.

Begin with the obvious things first:

The field in which you were educated. Do you have a college degree you are not using? Did you show a particular aptitude for something in school? Were you a whiz in algebra, winner of spelling bees?

Think of past jobs, even those you would rather forget! Include:

- High school or college activities such as helping produce the school yearbook or newspaper
- Planning parties for large groups
- Running a cash register

Hobbies. What do you do for fun?

- Flower arranging
- Reading aloud to young children
- Acting in community theater plays

Volunteer work. Where have you used your abilities to help others?

- Working with the disabled

- Hanging art exhibits
- Serving on a library committee

SURVIVAL TIP

If there is something you love to do, it is probably because you are good at it. Think back over the activities you have enjoyed doing, and you will have a quick overview of your abilities.

Dreaming Big

Take a close look at your Real World talents and skills. What do you see? Are there abilities there that you can combine, add to, and turn into a dream career?

- Ask yourself, "What in my wildest dreams would I like to do with the rest of my life?"
- Do not limit your thinking in any way.
- Set no parameters of time, money, or education. You are dreaming, and in dreams you do not have to worry about time, money, or education. Just *dream* and write. You can have more than one dream on the Dream side of the page. Perhaps two or three dreams on the list might be combined into an exciting career that makes you smile just to think of the possibility! The most important thing to remember as you do this process is to dare to dream and let your mind run rampant.
- On the Dream side of the page write those dreams down.
- Live with that list of dreams a few days.
- Determine which of these is your favorite dream. Is it attainable? *You bet it is!*

Attaining Your Dream Career

Determine your marketable skills. Determine which of your dreams, skills, and talents are marketable. Remember, a marketable skill is anything that people will pay you to do.

Let's just take one example and analyze it. Suppose you wrote on the Real World side that you have planned and organized parties. How is that a marketable skill?

Well, just think of the many activities that go into planning a successful party:

- Picking an appropriate time and place for a party
- Developing an invitation list
- Choosing or designing invitations
- Addressing and mailing invitations
- Creating a menu
- Ordering drinks or arranging a drink service
- Cooking and arranging food
- Decorating the room
- Organizing entertainment
- Troubleshooting during the party
- Greeting guests
- Introducing people
- Making people feel comfortable
- Creating order out of chaos when the party's over
- Paying the bills
- Writing thank-you notes

Now, who would find those party-giving skills marketable? Almost all of those specific activities are done by people who work in public relations, put on fund-raisers, and organize political campaigns. Nonprofit arts and cultural groups use those skills.

Texan Billie Byrd put her skills to work by starting a mailing company, Database Specialties. Her company created mailing lists, handled bulk mail, and organized huge mailings. She recently sold her lucrative business and became a marketing consultant to direct mail companies.

Byrd explained, "In college I majored in fashion merchandising, hoping to go into the retail business. But you have to be so good in design and I really wasn't. I started out in a small way, creating direct mail programs for churches and other businesses, just out of my home. In 1987 I was just about to open an office of my own when I found out I was expecting. I thought, what better career could I have with a baby? I worked for eighteen months out of my home until the computer equipment started overtaking the house. So I found a place where I could take my children and create a home away from home. We had a warehouse with 3200 square feet of space, so there was a place for tricycles, a VCR, everything kids need. I started hiring other moms who could bring their kids and we didn't have to worry about neatness or noise because it wasn't the kind of business where customers would walk in. All we had to be careful of was that the kids' fingerprints weren't on the mail. Finally Database Specialties became so big it outgrew me, and I sold it—very successfully."

Consider your skills and their career counterparts. If you have a degree in nuclear physics, it's pretty easy to figure out how to translate that into a job. But what about skills you have accumulated that are not as easy to put to use for pay?

Here are some examples of how some past experience can be used:

- **Babysitting.** Child care, adult day care, starting special programs such as a storytelling service at the local library, developing activities for very young children for museums and community theaters.
- **Spelling and reading.** Copyreading and editing newspapers, magazines, books. Checking technical reports for companies before they are printed.
- **Tennis.** Teaching tennis at the local racquet club, YMCA, YWCA, Girls Club and Boys Club, or Kids College. Working as a private tutor offering videotaped tennis sessions.
- **Gourmet cooking.** Catering, supervising cooking at projects such as "Meals on Wheels," teaching adult education classes at the local junior college, giving cooking demonstrations, starting a line of your own gourmet items in conjunction with a specialty store.
- **Dancing.** Teaching dancing lessons at a local school or for an organization, choreographing dance routines, leading a "dance for exercise" class, teaching dance therapy classes.

SKILLS WORKSHEET D

REAL WORLD (Skills I have now)	DREAM (New career/lifework)

Steps to Find My Dream (Skills to attain or obstacles to overcome)

1.
2.
3.
4.

Susie Hitchcock-Hall combined her two loves, cooking and dancing, to create "Susie's South 40 Candy," a wholesale candy-making company on forty acres of ranch land. When she isn't cooking up huge orders of chocolate-almond bark, Susie teaches country-western dancing in the rustic-looking building. During breaks in the music, she serves tiny slivers of her rich candy to her students. By the end of their lessons, they're as hooked on the candy as they are on the two-step. Just under a year old,

Susie's South 40 Candy is now shipped all over the United States and sold by catalogue, by phone, and in specialty stores.

Set a course of action. It's time to consider a course of action for attaining your dream. Do you need a few additional skills, such as computer literacy or a public-speaking course, to make your dream come true? List those skills needed on the bottom of the worksheet, under the heading "Steps to Find My Dream." Remember, Barbara needed to learn to use a computer, research marketing for a seminar, network with seminar presenters, and brush up on public speaking. Write down anything that will enhance your skills and help you make your dream come true.

There are a number of books written by women who started their own businesses. A few that might help you get started are *101 Best Small Businesses for Women* by Priscilla Y. Huff (Prima Publishing, 1996); *Dive Right In—The Sharks Won't Bite,* by Jane Wesman (Prentice Hall, 1995); *Our Wildest Dreams,* by Joline Godfrey (Harper Business, 1992), and *On Your Own,* by Laurie B. Zuckerman (Upstart Publishing, 1993).

Now go for it. Make your dream your priority. Make your dream your goal. You're ready for the next chapter, "Setting and Accomplishing Goals."

7

Setting and Accomplishing Your Goals

YOUR DREAM GOAL AND FINANCIAL ASSISTANCE

Pam, a suddenly single mother of two children, had been out of the workforce for twelve years. Pam's only work experience had been in retail sales—for a period of less than a year—after marrying Barry upon graduation from high school. Barry had died in an automobile accident a few months prior to her enrolling in our workshop.

Pam participated in our "Personal Bank Account of Life Experiences" workshop exercise and was sure she wanted a college degree and career in interior design. Skills and talents discovered and developed in high school home economics courses, short courses at the community college, and lots of volunteer decorating projects confirmed that this was her dream career, and one for which she was a natural.

Pam's biggest problem was a financial one. Through determination in seeking financial aid resources to help, Pam achieved her goal. She stayed near friends and family for the first two years at a local college, then relocated to a university town to complete her degree.

Pam urges others to be patient—working, going to school,

and being a single mom isn't easy, and you won't get through school as quickly as a carefree single college coed. It took almost seven years, but Pam is now a happily and lucratively employed interior designer! Pam has six tips for others:

1. Do you need more training—either on-the-job-training or help in going back to school? Look in your phone book white pages for "Job Training Partnership." This agency is in the business of helping people reenter the workforce or go back to school.
2. Be open to attaining vocational skills—such as computer literacy—that will allow you to get a better-paying job while you are working your way through college to earn your dream degree.
3. Call your local college or university for a step-by-step explanation of what is available in the way of scholarships.

SURVIVAL TIP

Need to work your way through college? Learn computer skill that will allow you to get a better-paying job while you're working your way through. Word-processing skills will be invaluable when you're in college—and for the rest of your life!

---

4. From child day care to housing assistance, your local United Way is an excellent resource for referring you to the proper social service organization to meet your needs. Call the United Way and explain your situation.
5. Many cities and communities publish a Directory of Community Services. Social services available in the local area are described in the directory, along with a phone number for each agency or not-for-profit organization. Call your local chamber of commerce, United Way, or Junior League to learn where you can get a copy or listing of available community services.
6. If you or a family member need some professional counseling to help you through this tough time, call your church for a

referral, or call your local mental health organization. Not-for-profit hospices offer counseling and support groups for adults and children who have suffered loss through death or divorce.

FINDING THE TIME

DONNETTE: *If you've just taken inventory of your skills and experiences in the preceding chapter and discovered that you do have a dream goal but feel a bit overwhelmed by the immense task of accomplishing that dream goal, take heart in the fact that you're not alone. All of us have had wishes and dreams that we just can't seem to get around to. Obstacles seem to multiply daily. Finding another minute to do another thing seems impossible.*

Barbara and I found ourselves in this dilemma back in the late spring of 1989. We were dreaming of starting a seminar business. We'd been through a lot of adversity ourselves, and wanted to help other women who were finding themselves suddenly alone without a man in the house—or his income! Barbara and I loved public speaking and yearned for an opportunity to teach and motivate other women to know that should they need to, they can make it on their own.

We were having a tough time motivating ourselves to get started writing our first seminar. We were both employed in other jobs—jobs which demanded sixty-plus hours a week—and time to write seemed nonexistent. We had told friends and family of our seminar business dream, including Barbara's daughter, Tricia, who was employed by a large Texas hospital as community events director.

Barbara's phone rang early one morning in May 1989, and it was Tricia. "Mom, you and Donnette better get busy. You're the program for a 'Women in Transition' workshop on October 17th."

"October 17th?" Our breaths collectively caught in our throats every time we repeated the date. "No way." "We don't have time." "How can we even think of starting a seminar business at age forty-eight?" "What if we bomb?"

After a ten-minute period of hand-wringing and pacing the floor, we realized that if we wanted our dream to come true, there had to be a way. We decided to start thinking positively. "We can make the time." "We'll never know if we're going to be good at this seminar business until we take a try at it." "Others have taken on new ventures at our age."

So Barbara and I turned to the method of problem solving that had helped us so often in the past: (1) Say a prayer. (2) Grab a pencil and paper. (3) Make a plan and write it down.

SURVIVAL TIP

You're never too old. Grandma Moses didn't start painting until she was eighty years old. Golda Meir was seventy-one when she became prime minister of Israel. Ruth Kells traveled to almost every country in the world after she was sixty-five, and at age ninety she was leading exercise classes for "old people."

MAKING A PLAN

We knew we had to be quite specific with our written plan. We knew that for several years we would need to continue working at our present jobs in order to put food on the table, but knew that ultimately we wanted our seminar and consulting business to be our main source of income. We did some research into how to draw up a plan to accomplish goals, then came forth with a simple format that made the most sense to us. At the end of the chapter is a worksheet for you to plan how you will accomplish your dream goal.

We started by writing down our goal, a broad statement of what we wanted to accomplish:

Goal: *We wish to be presenters of motivational seminars.*

Objectives: Next came the objectives under our goal. Our objectives were more specific, telling exactly what we will do, when we will do it, and how we will know it is a success.

Objective I. *We will plan, write, and present the motivational* seminar *"Women in Transition" by October 17, 1989. Success to be determined by our presenting the seminar to Methodist Hospital Lifestyles Group the evening of October 17, 1989, with a 90 percent positive evaluation report from evaluation sheets.*

Objective II. *We will formulate a marketing plan by February 15, 1990. Success of this objective to be measured by its completion by targeted date.*

Because our time was so precious, we had to have a specific plan of action. We wanted to express exactly how we were going to do what we wanted to do. We then had to allocate our resources, which are money, people, time, materials, and authority.

Plan of Action: *We will meet a least three hours a week, preferably on Sunday afternoons, for four months to write the seminar and to review what we might have gotten done on our own during the week before. After the seminar is written, we will meet for at least two hours a week for two months to practice with each other. We will use our friends as a "trial audience" and ask them to offer constructive criticism.*

Allocation of Resources:

- Money: *The only money needed at this time would be for pencils and yellow pads! Ten dollars maximum. If the seminar was favorably received, we would draw up a marketing plan.*
- People: *Barbara and Donnette. Later, ask six or eight friends to critique the seminar.*
- Time: *Stated above in Plan of Action.*
- Materials: *Yellow pads and pencils.*
- Authority: *Barbara and Donnette as partners have the authority. Seek professional marketing and tax advice after success of seminar is determined.*

We wanted an alternate plan, in case our main plan for formulating the seminar should break down. Then we would do what we said we were going to do, or execute the plan we'd devised. Finally, we would evaluate our seminar and write down what we would do differently next time.

Develop Alternate Plan: *Prefer to work on Sunday afternoons.*

Will work in late afternoon after work if we are falling behind, or if we miss a Sunday afternoon. Have extra names on the list of friends in case the first six or eight cannot be there.

Execute the Plan: *Write and practice, then perform the seminar October 17.*

Evaluation:

- **Did we accomplish what we wanted to do?** *We are delighted at the response, both personally and from the evaluation sheets. The answer is yes!*
- **How well did we use our resources?** *Our resources were our time, our friends' time, our pencils, and our legal pads. We evaluate that we used these resources well. We know that we could save a great deal of time if we had word-processing skills, however, and vow to sign up for a computer course immediately.*
- **Next time what would we do differently?** *We will have an anonymous question-and-answer period, because participants were reluctant to ask personal questions aloud. Instead, they waited until after the seminar and stormed the front of the room to ask their questions more privately. We will allow time at the end of the seminar for participants to write down their questions and then pass the hat to collect the questions. The questions can then be read aloud and answered for the benefit of all.*

SURVIVAL TIP

Fantasize! Imagine yourself in your dream goal; know that you *can* do it! Motivator Tony Robbins says: "If you believe you can't, you're probably right" (but only because your belief becomes a self-fulfilling prophecy).

HOW TO GET GOING: THREE JUMP-START TIPS

1. Tell a friend about your goal. Here's Kathy's story: For two years Kathy Rhodes's New Year's resolution had been to take a course that would teach her how to use the spreadsheet on her computer so she could handle all her family's bill paying. But she just couldn't seem to get around to it. She could have

---

SURVIVAL TIP

There is not a champion in the world who has not faced temporary defeat.

---

eventually forgotten it, but she made one mistake. She told a good friend, Suzy, about it. Every time she saw Suzy, she'd hear, "Kathy! How's your computer course coming?" and she'd have to admit she hadn't even registered for it yet. The Wednesday before she knew she'd be seeing Suzy at a luncheon, Kathy marched into the college continuing-education office and signed up. Months later, Kathy laughingly told Suzy, "Thank heaven I slipped and told you about my computer course resolution! If it hadn't been for you, I might never have bitten the bullet and signed up for the course. And that course has helped our entire family to budget better!"

2. Be patient with yourself. Mark Victor Hansen said, "Life is a marathon, not a sprint." Your goal may be a very long-term one, like Pam's desire to become an interior designer. If it's your dream goal, it's worth the work and the waiting.

3. Finally, be grateful for the blessings you have and the accomplishments you make as you're fulfilling your dream. If you're having trouble feeling grateful, rent a video movie about Helen Keller's life.

MAKING A PLAN WORKSHEET

GOAL: Broad statement of what you want to accomplish:

- Objectives: More specific statements telling what you will do, when you will do it, and how you will know it is a success. There may be as many objectives under your goal as you wish.
- Objective I
- Objective II

Make a Plan for Allocation of Resources

- Money
- People
- Time
- Materials
- Authority

Develop Alternate Plan (in case main plan should break down)
Execute the Plan
Evaluate the Outcome

- Did I accomplish what I wanted to do?
- How well did I use my resources?
- What should I do differently next time?

8

Landing a Job or
Starting a Business

It was all Carol could do to sit still during the first half hour of
the "Jobs and Careers" workshop. The look of fatigue in her eyes
and the rigid set of her shoulders spelled "fear for financial
survival." At break time Carol admitted, "If the local YWCA
hadn't sponsored this workshop free of charge, I couldn't have
come. I need to know how to go about finding a better-paying
job, but my mind has been in such shock I can't think how to
begin."

Break time ended and the workshop resumed. As Carol
progressed through the assessment of skills in her personal bank
account of life experiences (chapter 6) and participated in the
goal-setting exercise (chapter 7), we began to see an occasional
ray of hope gleaming in her eyes. At lunch break, Carol said, "I'm
encouraged, and I'm feeling a lot more organized now, but can
we get down to the nuts and bolts now? You know, the details of
how I do my resumé and go about interviewing and actually
finding a job."

"Absolutely," we promised. "Right after the lunch break, we'll
go into each detail."

For many women, being suddenly single means that they are

in the market for a job, either for the first time, or in the search for a better job because of their newly constrained budgets. You may be searching for an interim job to put you through college, a job to give you on-the-job training toward a career goal, or you may be reaching for the perfect next step up the ladder of your dream career.

If your goal is to one day have a business of your own, we're certainly all for you! We have some tips for you in the latter part of this chapter. One tip is that we strongly recommend that you acquire considerable experience in the business of your dreams prior to starting your own business in that field. For instance, Barbara and I had extensive public-speaking and administrative experience before we started our seminar business. We held several jobs which gave us that experience.

FINDING A JOB

We found that there are six basic steps to becoming employed:

1. Assessing your skills and needs;
2. Networking;
3. Formulating a resumé;
4. Writing a personalized cover letter for each resumé;
5. Interviewing;
6. Considering the offer.

Assessing Your Skills and Needs

- Do some honest soul-searching. Look back at your worksheet in chapter 6, "Your Personal Bank Account of Life Experiences." Remember to put away self-doubt and false modesty! Decide which skills you want to market, and be honest with yourself about the areas in which you need more expertise or training.
- If you need more training—either on-the-job training or a college degree—or if you need help in locating a job or financial assistance to aid you in going back to school, read again Pam's tips found in the "Your Dream Goal and Financial Assistance" section of chapter 7, "Setting and Accomplishing Your Goals."

- Consider your personal preferences and needs. Do you prefer to work alone because you are a self-starter and are adept at managing your time? Or are you more productive under supervision? Do you prefer working with other people? Are you free to travel?
- What are your income needs? Do you prefer the security of a salaried position, or are you more motivated when you're working on commission? Have you considered a combination of both salary and commission?
- Would you have to move to a different location to find the type of work you want? Do you need to stay in your present location, say, for the sake of the children, or are you free to move to a different location to find your dream job? Get an idea from your state employment office about local rates of pay as compared to rates of pay in a different location. Bear in mind that the cost of living, such as housing, taxes, and even groceries, may be higher in a different city.

Networking

- How do you find a new hairdresser or a different gynecologist? You ask your friends for referrals! Begin your job search the same way. Ask family, friends, and professional, religious, or fraternal organization acquaintances for recommendations. Ask them to keep you in mind and call you if they hear about any jobs in your field. If you don't hear from them, call them back, so they will remember you are in the market for a job.
- Make a list of companies for which you might like to work. If possible, talk to some employees of the companies on your list to seek further information. Inquire if this is a company they intend to stay with. If the employee is not happy there, perhaps this is a company you would not wish to pursue. If details such as working conditions, pay and benefits sound satisfactory, ask who would be doing the hiring for the position you are seeking. Ask friends, family, and acquaintances if they know of anyone who works for the companies on your list so you might use your friends' names to introduce yourself in your cover letter.

- Each day check the newspaper classified sections.
- Let your state employment service know that you are in the market for a job.
- Register with your college placement office.
- Check with professional employment agencies about their fee requirements. The trend is toward the fees to be paid by the employer; however, the person seeking the employment is still charged by some agencies, while other agencies allow the fee to be split between the applicant and employer. Depending upon your situation, you may wish to enlist the services of an employment agency.
- Barbar's son-in-law, Joe, made us aware that on the Internet, there are many quality job banks and job postings available. He urged us to tell our seminar participants to use one of the major search engines to help locate job banks and job postings.
- Read, read, read. Business magazines and newspaper business sections feature businesses that are new and expanding. The chamber of commerce may have a business directory or monthly journal.

Writing Your Resumé

SURVIVAL TIP

Do include volunteer jobs in your resumé. Be sure to describe the jobs so that they reflect the skills you used to get the job done.

- Be concise. This is not a narrative autobiography. Omit personal data such as age, height, marital status, and year you graduated (especially for the older applicant). Many employers do not discriminate against older people, but our seminar participants tell us that there are still some who do. Do not use the word *resumé* at the top. Give your full name. Do not use nicknames unless it is absolutely necessary for identification. Include a mailing address, phone number, and, if applicable, a fax number.

JANE DOE SMITH ——————————

123 Worthington Lane   Telephone   (123) 456-7890
Anywhere, US 99999   FAX   (123) 456-7890

JOB OBJECTIVE

> A middle management position in the field of health care, such as a hospital, governmental health agency, or community clinic, or a managerial development position with a health-related not-for-profit organization.

EXPERIENCE

> **Executive Director, Anywhere USA Health & Retirement Endeavor**
> Responsible for:
> Health referral services for retirees and their families.
> Educational seminars for residents.
> National marketing to attract retirees to the area.
> Organizing and supervising all fund-raising activities.
> Formulating yearly budget for approval by Board of Directors.
> Presentation of yearly funding requests to City Council.
> Public-speaking presentation to community groups regarding programs and progress of the organization
>
> **Muscular Dystrophy Chairman, Anywhere, USA**
> Organized and implemented all-city fund drive by recruiting and training 70 volunteers.
> Public speaking and media presentations to advertise the event.
>
> **FACT Event Coordinator**
> Recruited volunteers, raised funds, and wrote letter to bring Mrs. Betty Ford to Anywhere to speak on the topic, "Substance Abuse: A Family Illness."
> Public speaking and media presentations to advertise the event.

Hospice of Anywhere

One of five-member Steering Comittee to establish Hospice of Anywhere.

Public presentations to community to introduce concept of Hospice.

Worked closely with hospitals and community physicians to introduce the concept of Hospice, and to maintain good public relations.

Wrote initial bylaws of Hospice of Anywhere.

Researched and wrote management section of original Policies and Procedures Manual.

Helped to organize and served on original Board of Directors; continued to serve on Board of Directors and Executive Committee for five years.

Organized and implemented Friends of Hospice fund-raising drive, raising $82,000 the first year; increasing income by 15% to 35% each year for five years.

President, Board of Directors

Clearview Hospital

Secretary-Treasurer, Board of Directors

Responsible for financial reports presented monthly to Board of Directors.

EDUCATION

Principles of Supervision: A two-semester course, Anywhere, USA College, 5 Credits.

Office Management: Philosophy and Techniques of Business, Anywhere, USA College, 5 Credits.

Commercial National Bank, Anywhere USA, Audit/Management Training (a one-year on-the-job training course).

Bachelor of Arts, French and Spanish, Anywhere University

Five Spanish courses in one semester, University of the Americas, Mexico City.

INTERESTS

Tennis, Hiking, Reading, Bilingual Volunteering

- Be organized.
- List your job objective. Be as general as possible so as not to miss out on any opportunities for interviewing in your field.
- List your education and training. Education should be the first qualification listed *if* it is essential to your job objectives; for instance, if you are applying for a job as an accountant, your accounting education background is important. If you are seeking a job in fund-raising and your formal education is in elementary education, then first list all the experience you have had in the field of fund-raising. Include all types of education and training you have received, regardless of whether it is for credit or noncredit. If your education dates are fairly recent, include them; if not, omit the dates.
- List your places of employment and volunteer work. Be results oriented in describing your jobs. Be specific about what you accomplished in each job.
- It is appropriate to say "References supplied upon request," if you wish. Names of references may be included with the resumé, but should be on a separate sheet of paper.
- Include personal information such as hobbies and sports, if you wish.
- Proofread, proofread! Be sure that your resumé is of professional quality with absolutely no mistakes.

Writing a Cover Letter

- Address the letter to whoever will be making the hiring decision.
- Early in the letter, show that you are familiar with the company or organization to which you are applying.
- Concentrate on your skills. Be specific and show how your skills will be of benefit to each company. For instance, show how you can save the company money or improve public relations. Do not label yourself with a title, as you could be unconsciously limiting your abilities in the eyes of the person doing the hiring.
- Within the bounds of good taste and etiquette, the cover letter needs to be as distinctive as possible, so that your resumé will be remembered in a positive way. Early in her career, Barbara

Jane Doe Smith

123 Worthington Lane, Anywhere, US 99999   Telephone 123/456-7890   Fax 123/456-7891

May 1, 1998

Mr. Henry Jones
Administrator
Anywhere Memorial Hospital
Any Street
Anywhere, USA 99990

Dear Mr. Jones:

It was with much pleasure that I noted your advertisement for a Development Director for Memorial Hospital's Foundation Fund. Enclosed is my resumé in application for the position. As you may see from my resumé, my administrative and fund-raising experience has been predominantly in the not-for-profit health sector.

As Executive Director of the Anywhere Health and Retirement Endeavor for the past four years, I have succeeded in increasing its funding by 250 percent and its volunteer participation threefold. Other fund-raising successes are noted in the resumé. I am a people person and I like training and motivating others to action.

Anywhere Memorial Hospital enjoys an excellent reputation. Through the years, Memorial has met the health needs of my family in a most professional and caring manner. I would be honored to be associated with such a fine institution.

I would very much like to interview for the position of Development Director, and appreciate your consideration of my qualifications.

Sincerely,

Jane Doe Smith

Enclosure

was searching statewide, sending out her resumé to not-for profit organizations in search for a job as a development (fund-raising) consultant. Barbara's cover letter was on quality white stationery with large apple-green personalized letterhead reading BARBARA TOM JOWELL. After about two weeks, Barbara would call her contact at each organization to inquire if her resumé had been received. "My cover letter was the one with the apple-green letterhead, if you will remember," she would carefully remind those who were unsure as to whether the resumé had been received. "Oh, yes, we certainly remember getting that—an excellent resumé and letter," was generally the encouraging reply. A couple of the recipients chuckled, "The green letterhead print made us think of all the cash you'd be able to raise for us!" Bear in mind that green letterhead print might not be appropriate for all cover letters—such as a dignified law firm or banking institution.

- When you check back to inquire if the resumé has been received, ask if you may set an appointment for a personal interview.

Interviewing

Elizabeth, an executive vice president of marketing for a midsize manufacturing firm, joined us for lunch one day. "I'm so disappointed," she sighed, pulling out her chair. "Judging by the applicant's resumé, I thought I would be interviewing the perfect person for a sales position this morning. But she arrived late, breathless and disheveled with no particular apology or excuse. And it seemed as if she'd never even glanced at the job description in the newspaper. If she's always this scatterbrained, we just can't take a chance with her."

Remember that the company needs just the right person just as much as you need the right job! Do your homework prior to the interview and project an enthusiastic, positive attitude during the interview.

Before the Interview

- Research the company as well as you can. Try to get quarterly or annual reports.

- Try to get the job description.
- Anticipate questions you may be asked, such as the minimum salary you require, your expectations of the job, why you feel you are the best person for this job, your attitude about working long hours, or your willingness to relocate.
- Call to reconfirm your appointment time and place. This is a good time to ask if you could get a copy of the exact job description, if you do not already have one.
- After you have read the job description, make a list of questions you might like to ask about the job, such as any gray areas about reimbursable expenses, time requirements, or amount of travel involved.

A day or more before the interview, find the address and exact location of the office within the building where you will be interviewing. If you are driving your own car, will parking be a problem? Make a note of the travel time to and from the office. Pick up the job description and use this opportunity to take note of the apparent appropriate dress code, if possible.

The night before, organize your wardrobe, including all accessories. Create a professional appearance. Plan to dress appropriately to the position for which you are interviewing. Put an extra pair of hose in your purse.

The Day of the Interview

- Allow more than adequate time for dressing and travel.
- Arrive a few minutes early.
- Use a firm handshake.
- Make eye contact.
- Keep a positive attitude, and project a confident image.
- Be concise, elaborating on replies only when asked to do so.
- If you do not know the answer to a question, say so. If you are asked a question that would require some time to consider, such as, "Would you consider working on a consulting basis, rather than as a full-time employee?" do not feel that you must answer immediately. Smile, and say, "That is certainly a consideration. Do you mind if I give it a little thought and perhaps talk it over with my accountant?"

- If the interviewer does not indicate a time frame, ask, "When will you be needing someone to fill the position?"

After the Interview

- Immediately write a thank-you note to the interviewer.
- If there are currently no jobs available, call back every few weeks to ask about new openings.

Considering an Offer

When you are offered a job, be sure that you understand the details of the offer. For instance, how long before you are vested in the pension plan? How exactly is the commission figured? Is sick leave offered? Are there any personal days off? What specifically are the holidays? Be sure that you understand these details and any others that are of importance to you. Many employers are accustomed to submitting their offers in writing, so you (after expressing your pleasure at being offered the job) may feel free to ask politely, "I am a little foggy on some of the details of the offer. Would you mind sending me a written offer, so I may get everything straight in my mind?" A fair-minded employer will not take offense at such a request.

Above all, be patient. You will find a job, and ultimately you'll be in the career of your dreams!

STARTING YOUR OWN BUSINESS

In our workshop "Finding a Job or Starting Your Own Business," we urge our participants to work at least two years as an employee in the career of their dreams before starting a business of their own. In other words, we advise them, "Make your mistakes while working for someone else!" About a year and a half after Betty had attended one of our workshops, we got this letter from her:

Dear Donnette and Barbara:

My mother used to say, "The road to hell is paved with good intentions." Mom certainly pegged me in more ways than one.

I finally followed through on my first good intention. I finally got around to taking your mini-seminar about starting one's own business. I was so fired up about starting my catering business. The first fifteen minutes of the seminar, I was smug. I had met your criteria of working in my field before I started a business. I'd worked for a local caterer for four years. I was convinced that anything he could do, I could do better. My recipes were better, and my service and presentation could put his in the shade.

The next portion of the workshop—well, I hated every word of what I heard. My eyes rolled back in my head with all that gibberish about business plans, bank loans, cash flow. How dumb. I had saved some money, not much, but some. Why should I do a business plan? I wasn't about to mess with all that paperwork. Then you said, "If it's worth your life's blood in time and money, it's worth a couple months of planning for it on paper. Do a business plan."

A business plan sounded like I'd been sentenced to writing War and Peace *in Latin, but I slept on the idea. Actually I nightmared about it. "It's not necessary to do a business plan unless I run out of money and have to go to the bank," whispered one little jagged voice. "Oh yes it is," would scream the voice of my common sense.*

At last I followed through on my second good intention. I called the Small Business Development Center, and went to one of their seminars. Then one of those wonderful people helped walk me through my business plan. I did end up having to ask my folks for some money, and the bank for a little more. But I had a plan, a lot of determination, and I'm now showing a profit. Thank you for being my tough mentors.

Warmest regards,

Betty Case
Case Catering

Business Plans and Business Savvy

We said it before, and it deserves repeating: If you're considering starting your own business, work as an employee in that field for at least two years and gain substantial experience before attempting to start your own business. If you have labored in the field of your dreams and still are firmly convinced that you want a business of your own, you will need to do all in your power to assure its success.

Be realistic! The grim truth is that there are more new businesses that are failures than there are new businesses that are successful. Do as much planning on paper as you can to find out whether your business has a chance of success. You will need to learn how to develop a business plan, which is the description of your company and a plan of how it will function. You will need a business plan and a financial statement if you need to seek funding. Realize that you will probably not show a profit for three years and must be able to sustain your livelihood and that of your employees for that period of time.

Even if you do not need to seek outside funding, a business plan is essential to helping you organize your thoughts and be realistic about the goals for your company. The business plan will force you to explain the market for your product, will show that you are aware of your competition and how you will produce your product and market it better than your competition. The plan will show the organization of your business and its personnel. Financial information such as three years' projected sales and expenses for equipment, supplies, and staff, as well as cash flow for three years, will be included. The plan will reflect the amount of funding you expect to need and will include a time format for break-even and profit making.

Funding

In addition to doing a business plan, you will need to consider funding. If you do not have your own funding, you will need to seek a loan, which will probably require you to put up some type of collateral (to guarantee the loan will be repaid) if you have no proven success in your business field. Here are a few tips on how to educate yourself on starting your new business:

Call your local Small Business Development Center. The number should be in the white pages of your phone book. Services offered by the Small Business Development Centers include free seminars and one-on-one counseling on:

- Business plans
- Marketing strategies
- Record keeping
- Cash flow management
- Tax planning
- Business law

Call your local chamber of commerce. Chambers of commerce are in the business of attracting and retaining new businesses within your community. Many chambers can give referrals to sources to help with business plans, marketing strategies, and networking, and also may have the latest information on local funding for new businesses. Many chambers have a library of educational videos for new entrepreneurs.

Call your local college or university to find out about continuing-education courses for new entrepreneurs. Find out what the college knows about what is available locally to assist the new-business owner.

Look into funding. The Small Business Administration (SBA) is expanding a pilot program launched two years ago to help women prequalify for loans. This precertification program will in effect guarantee loans before women entrepreneurs approach lenders. Applicants will be required to submit a detailed business plan, along with a statement of their finances. To locate the Small Business Administration office nearest you, look in the white pages under "United States Government." If there is no office in your town, call 1-800-8-ASK-SBA (1-800-827-5722).

Many big banks have begun special loan programs aimed at

minorities and women. Call the commercial loan departments of your local banks to inquire. Bear in mind, most programs do require some type of collateral.

For small loans, seek out nonprofit sources, such as Accion Internacional. After years of offering microloans to entrepreneurs throughout Latin America, Accion is opening offices in the United States. Accion requires that your business be functional for at least a year. After a year, small loans, typically for around one thousand dollars, may be granted. Loans are for a short period of time, generally about six months, and interest rates are high, close to 16 percent. The nonprofit group says the rate reflects the high cost of making a large number of small loans.

Starting Small

When starting your own business, consider starting small, then expanding. Barbara's daughter, Shelley, saw a need for stationery for children. She couldn't find it anywhere! Shelley located several popular sources of children's stationery and started a small business out of her home. She advertised locally and by word of mouth to friends, and the orders began pouring in.

Within a short period of time, Shelley's clients started asking for other items. "Could you order wedding invitations?" "I need some enclosure cards." "Do you think you could find some really unique party invitations?" Shelley began ordering more and more types of catalogues to fill the needs of her expanding clientele. Before long, Shelley's catalogue inventory outgrew her home, and she relocated to a small shop in a shopping center, taking care to keep her overhead in check.

Shelley's success story is not just a matter of good luck. Good luck comes as a result of doing your homework, being aware of your competition, being sufficiently funded, and being willing to work tenaciously toward your goal. We wish you every success!

9

The Professionals You Work With

DONNETTE: *After Mac died, I contacted the life insurance companies. Benefits of two of the life insurance policies were paid immediately. A third company said they'd hand-deliver my benefits check. I assured them that wasn't necessary, but they insisted, "It's standard procedure for us to have someone deliver the check. One of our people will be in your area within a week." As one week stretched into another, I got more and more anxious, fearing that perhaps they were trying to find a way to keep from paying Mac's life insurance benefits to me. A man from the life insurance company would call, apologize for the delay, and say he'd be there on a different date. Then a few days later I'd hear, "Something came up—couldn't make it. So sorry."*

Finally, he called to say he was in town; we made an appointment to meet at a local restaurant, and the check was hand-delivered. At long last I learned the reason he wanted personally to bring the money. He was determined to persuade me that his company would be the best to invest the money for me. I grasped for a quick excuse, finally stammering something about needing a variety of professional advice before I made any

123

firm decisions, thanked him, escaped, and breathed a sigh of relief. Then I set out to do just that—find some good professional advice.

When transition occurs, whether through divorce or death, one of the first decisions a woman must make is about the professionals who will advise her. This material deals with the who, what, when, where, and how of choosing and working with advisers.

- *Who?* Attorneys, accountants, financial planners, and insurance agents will be discussed. The following questions will be answered.
- *When* do I need an adviser?
- *Where* do I begin to look for an adviser?
- *What* should be the criteria for choosing them?
- *How much* should I expect to pay? *How* do I interview?

GENERAL RULES FOR CHOOSING AN ADVISER

Here are some general rules for choosing any adviser or agent:

- Ask your friends and colleagues with needs similar to your own for their recommendations.
- Has the adviser had experience? A good rule of thumb is to choose an adviser who has had at least three years' experience in the field. Choose advisers by their experience with cases or situations similar to yours.
- Think twice before using friends or relatives. Would you even be considering that person as your adviser if he or she were not your friend or relative? Would you get the same treatment as a client whose relationship with your adviser was purely professional?
- Check on potential advisers' credentials—professional degrees, memberships, and designations. A title does not guarantee competence, but it does show that they have cared enough to do extra study of the subject.
- Request a free-of-charge consultation. If the adviser will not consent to this, first interview those who will. If an adviser is

highly recommended by friends and colleagues, he or she may be worth the cost of a consultation fee. Do not refuse to interview him or her just because a consultation fee is required.

- Will the adviser handle your business personally, or will it be transferred to a junior partner? With whom will you deal when your adviser is ill or out of town?
- What are the fees? Are fees negotiable? Will the adviser give you a written estimate of the total cost? Can special payment schedules be arranged to fit your budget needs? Will the adviser put your agreement in writing?
- Will the adviser supply you with references?
- Advisers are only as good as the information you supply to them. Be willing to do your homework and prepare thoroughly for each meeting.
- Advisers should be willing to work with each other to your overall benefit. Ask the adviser if he or she would be willing to interact with your CPA, your lawyer for wills, estate planning and tax strategies, the mortgage bankers/broker, and trust company officers.

ATTORNEYS

When to Call a Lawyer

You should consider calling a lawyer if you are in any of the following situations:

- Signing complex contracts for large amounts of money.
- Starting a new business. You should protect your personal assets from any business creditors, get information as to whether to incorporate, and be sure to set up measures to avoid liability for any injuries your employees may sustain.
- Resolving complicated tax problems with the Internal Revenue Service (IRS). Consult a tax attorney.
- Making a will. One of the first things you need to do when divorcing or becoming a widow is to make a new will. Details to consider when making a will are included in chapter 10, "Protecting Your Assets." Standard fees range from $75 to

$1,500, depending on the complexity of the will and where you live.

- Guiding an estate through probate. Some advice suggests that an attorney is not necessary for a very simple estate; however, we advise that you seek advice of counsel for general guidelines. To keep fees at a minimum, you can do a lot of the detail work for the attorney. Details on settling the estate and duties of an executor are included in chapter 3, "Widowed." If a widow is comfortable using the attorney who drew up her husband's will, he would be the logical one to use to guide the estate through probate; however, if there is a potential conflict of interest because that attorney also represents her late husband's business, another attorney should represent the interests of the estate. It is usually preferable to choose an attorney whose fee is based on an hourly rate, rather than a fee based on a percentage of the estate. Remember to get a written estimate first!

- Buying or selling a house. Details to consider in buying or selling a house are included in chapter 12, "New Car Fever." Depending on fees in your area of the country, and the amount of time the contract requires, expect a fee of $250 to $600. In some states, attorneys charge a percentage of the mortgage or sale price of the house.

- Finding out whether you are entitled to be compensated for injuries. If you are injured by tripping over an electrical cord negligently left in the middle of the floor in the beauty shop, you could be compensated for your lost wages, doctor bills, and your pain and suffering. If you're injured on the job, you may be eligible for workman's compensation or social security disability.

- Being called to court as a defendant. Legal representation is guaranteed by the Constitution to all people who are accused of a crime. If you can't afford an attorney, the court will appoint one for you.

- Having serious financial difficulty and needing advice as to bankruptcy filing.

- Getting a divorce. Some information you read might suggest a do-it-yourself divorce to save money. This might be possible if you have no children, you have been married for less than five years, there are few assets, and *you are able to communicate with each other.* We personally suggest that you use an attorney. A woman contemplating divorce should never use the same lawyer her husband uses. Detailed information on divorce is in chapter 2.

- Drafting a prenuptial agreement. Especially in a remarriage, you should consider this safeguard of your assets. (See chapter 14, "Socializing and Dating Again.")
- Facing job discrimination. If you believe that you have been treated unfairly due to your race, sex, religion, age, or a disability, consult an employment lawyer.

How to Choose and Interview an Attorney

When choosing an attorney, first ask your friends and colleagues for their recommendations. If you are new to the area, contact the city, county, or state bar association for names of lawyers dealing with your area of concern. If you live near a law school, call and ask if the school or faculty members could recommend someone to handle your specific problem.

When interviewing, ask about experience with cases or situations similar to yours. Ask for references. Then check those references carefully.

Ask how long the attorney has been with the current firm. Where was he or she employed before? Any distinctions or awards in a particular field of law?

Inquire about the fees. There are several ways lawyers charge:

- By the project or flat fee. As an example, $500 for a will.
- By the hour. The attorney may charge $125 for each hour of work, for example.
- Retainer. This is money that an attorney wants up front. It is like a deposit and is credited toward your final bill.
- Range fee. The attorney leaves the final fee open, not knowing how much work will be needed in your case. You are given a range of what you will pay, for example: between $1,000 and $5,000.
- Percentage fee. Often used in probate cases, where the at-

torney takes a percentage of the estate. (We advise that it is preferable to pay by the hour. Get an estimate first!)

- On contingency. There can be a contingency arrangement only in situations involving a monetary award. The attorney is paid a percentage of whatever your award is. The percentage amount—generally in the range of 20 to 50 percent—is negotiable. When negotiating the contingency percentage, remember: with a fixed agreement, the lawyer is paid the same percentage whether the case is settled in a meeting the very first week or takes months and goes all the way through a trial.

So inquire about flat fees, hourly rates, if a retainer is required, and, if applicable to your situation, contingency or percentage fees. Be sure you can get a written estimate of all costs before the attorney begins. Ask for monthly bills and ask that bills be itemized in detail.

Ask how long it should take to complete your case, and if you will be kept abreast at regular intervals as to the progress of your case.

Ask to meet the attorney who will handle your case when he or she is ill or out of town.

Find out if the attorney will consent to binding arbitration if there are differences between you. Arbitration means the parties give a third person the power to decide the dispute as a judge would. Binding arbitration means you agree beforehand to abide by the decision as if it were law.

As you interview the attorney, do you feel that you're being talked down to, or is he or she talking in legalese gobbledygook that you can't understand? If the answer to either of these questions is yes, then by all means, find another lawyer!

SURVIVAL TIP

Free legal assistance: If you have a very limited income you may qualify for legal help. To find a local office in your state, call the Legal Services Corporation at 1-202-336-8800.

TAX PREPARERS AND ACCOUNTANTS

SURVIVAL TIP

No matter who prepares your tax return, the IRS holds *you* responsible for its accuracy.

DONNETTE: *Unless there is a reason to do otherwise, a widow usually finds it easier to stay with the tax preparer she and her husband have employed in the recent past. I used the same accountant Mac and I had used for the six years prior to his death. This CPA (certified public accountant) was able to handle all the final tax returns in a timely manner because he was familiar with our financial situation.*

BARBARA: *On the other hand, I changed accountants immediately after my divorce because I wanted an accountant who had* my *best interests in mind, rather than my husband's. Each of us has to assess our own situation and make the decision that's most appropriate.*

The Volunteer Income Tax Assistance (VITA) program is sponsored by the IRS and offers free tax preparation to low-income, disabled, elderly or non-English-speaking persons who file simple returns. For the elderly, the IRS provides tax counseling, also staffed by trained volunteers, who will come to your home or a nursing home. Some of the tax counseling centers are organized by the American Association of Retired Persons (AARP), and are called Tax-Aide Centers.

High-volume tax service companies will prepare simple tax forms at a modest price. Some of these offices stay open year-round to answer tax questions, but it's hard to maintain a year-round client relationship with many of them.

Who Should Prepare Your Tax Return?

If your return is quite complicated, you will probably need a tax accountant or certified public accountant. Finding an experienced, competent tax preparer is critical. The accountant who prepares your taxes should be more than a bookkeeper. After he or she has prepared your return, you will need him or her to help you plan each year and make recommendations that are appropriate for you for the next year. It is important to get into the habit each year of reviewing where you are and where you are going. If your accountant does not have time to sit down and do this with you, then find another accountant. Tax laws change frequently so deal with someone who keeps abreast of changes and alerts you to any changes that affect you.

- Ask friends for their recommendations. If you are new to the area, call local and state associations of accountants for their referrals.
- If you need specific expertise (such as on landlord-tenant issues or oil and gas regulations), inquire if the preparer has experience in this field.
- If you are involved in tax disputes with the Internal Revenue Service, you will need a CPA, tax attorney, or enrolled agent. (An enrolled agent is a noncertified accountant who has passed an IRS test that qualifies him or her to act as an agent.) These professionals are expensive, usually charging $125 and up per hour. Like many attorneys, they also may charge by the hour when you are talking on the phone to them, so have your questions organized and well thought out when you contact them.
- Be sure that your tax preparer's office is open all year, and not just at tax time, because tax problems can occur at any time of the year. Ask if the preparer will accompany you to the IRS in case you are audited, to help explain how your return was prepared.

As with interviewing any adviser, ask how the tax preparer is compensated. Tax preparation can be a flat fee or on an hourly basis. Billing for an audit is usually on an hourly basis.

FINANCIAL PLANNERS

When to Hire a Financial Planner

Do you need some help analyzing your financial needs and planning for the future?

Do you think you might need professional advice or referral to professionals to help with estate planning, health, long-term care, or life insurance? Would you like to have a written financial plan, based on your needs—with help for implementing the plan with continuing consultations about the plan in the future? If any of the above criteria applies to you, you might want to enlist the services of a financial planner.

According to John H. Alpers, CFP, managing director of Gateway Financial Strategies LLC, of Boulder, Colorado, a registered investment adviser (RIA), the starting point for all financial planning is an inventory and analysis of your current position. You must be willing to take the time to fill in the blanks to furnish the information the planner will require, such as personal income tax returns for the past three years, your current will, current budget, a list of your assets and liabilities with copies of all bank, mutual fund, and investment statements, all life, health, disability, auto, home, and liability insurance policies, employee benefit plan statements, and all retirement fund statements. A competent planner should ask questions to guide you in analyzing your risk tolerance (how much risk you are willing to take with your investments), your future goals, and your retirement needs.

A good financial plan should help you identify your financial goals and then give you a plan as to how to attain your goals. According to Alpers, financial goals fall into six categories:

Standard of living. This is your desire to maintain an enjoyable standard of living under present and future income and economic conditions. It includes satisfactory allocations of funds to permit adequate food, clothing, and shelter in addition to a balance of luxury items.

Savings. You will require a certain amount of cash reserves for emergencies—usually three to six months' worth of expenses should be reserved for emergencies. Although liquidity is a requirement for contingency funds, this does not necessarily mean that all these funds need to be in a savings account.

Risk protection. It is important that you arrange for protection against insurable risks. You will want to insure against the potential loss not only of your physical properties, but also of future income through disability and loss of capital through personal liabilities, such as the costs of long-term rehabilitative/ custodial care in a nursing home.

Accumulation of investments. This is the most complex of financial goals, as it requires the determination of investment priorities and the choice from a wide variety of investment vehicles. It is important that you are able to quantify the amount and clearly define the time frame in which this is to happen. (More on investments in chapter 10, "Protecting Your Assets.")

Financial independence. This is the age at which you wish to retire and the amount of income per month (inflation-adjusted) that you will require to live as well as possible during your retirement years.

Estate planning. As wealth is accumulated, it is necessary to plan for its appropriate distribution in the event of death. Usually this goal also involves planning to ensure that your estate is adequately preserved in the event of your death.

The optimum financial plan will give you direction as to how to budget now and allocate your investments to achieve your financial goals. Suggestions may be made as to other needs. For instance, you may be reminded to update your will to save estate taxes, or to draw up a durable power of attorney for health care. (More on wills in chapter 10, "Protecting Your Assets.")

How to Choose a Financial Planner

Ask friends for their recommendations. For free information about financial planning and names of members in your area, call the Institute of Certified Financial Planners Consumer Assistance Line, 1-800-282-7526, or the International Association for Financial Planning, 1-800-945-4237. After you've come up with some names, call your local Better Business Bureau to be sure there have been no complaints against any of them.

Ask for credentials such as CFP, Certified Financial Planner, or ChFC, Chartered Financial Consultant (an insurance industry designation). Ask if he or she is registered with the federal

Securities and Exchange Commission (SEC) as a Registered Investment Adviser (RIA). Does he or she keep up with the latest tax, investment and financial-planning news? You should expect your planner to be available and willing to give you sufficient time for explaining information and making recommendations.

Ask whether the financial planner gets a fee, commission, or both. The cost of a financial plan can range from a few hundred dollars to a few thousand dollars, depending upon the complexity of your financial situation. For a flat fee, a fee-only financial planner will assist with your financial plan and give you advice on whether you need the help of attorneys, accountants, investment personnel, and insurance agents. The fee-only planner does not sell any type of investment products. A commission-only financial planner sells investment products and insurance and receives a commission from the company selling the products recommended. Be sure you trust the commission-only planner before investing in these products. If the planner works on commission, ask how many companies the financial planner represents and choose a planner with a wide range of choices— not just one or two—to meet your insurance, investment, and other needs.

A planner who is a combination fee-only and commission-only will probably charge a lower fee for the plan in the hope you will buy insurance or investment products from him or her.

Ask if he or she is a "captive agent" of one company. If the financial planner is also a broker-dealer representative who can help you modify or reconfigure your investment portfolio, it is far preferable that he or she should be able to offer products from a multitude of different vendors and principals.

Ask how your plan would be prepared. Would the planner use sophisticated computer software to help with the preparation of your plan? Would your plan be carefully analyzed as to your personal situation and future goals? Would you meet regularly throughout the year to follow the progress of your plan? Would the plan be reallocated and updated regularly, say quarterly, to monitor your investments and the other aspects of your financial situation?

Determine if this adviser will work with your other advisers. Ask, "Can and will you offer guidance on how to pursue and achieve legal, estate-planning, and tax goals, and will you work with my lawyer, estate-planner, and accountant?"

Be sure this adviser has the right kind of experience. Ask, "How many financial plans have you prepared for people in similar financial situations to my own?"

SURVIVAL TIP

"Beware of any financial planner who tends to look at the financial planning compendium through a prism which assumes that all the world's problems can be solved with one single type of investment."—John H. Alpers, CFP, managing director, Gateway Financial Strategies, Boulder, Colorado, a registered investment adviser (RIA)

INSURANCE AGENTS

How to Find an Insurance Agent

Ask friends with needs similar to your own for their recommendations. Insurance is sometimes very tedious. More than likely your first need in insurance will be for your home or your car, which is called "casualty insurance." Agents who specialize in casualty insurance usually offer disability and life insurance. However, agents who specialize in life insurance usually do not sell casualty. We recommend that you choose a casualty agent for home/car and then another for life insurance.

The insurance industry has had some problems lately, so you want to make sure that you select an agent who represents a company with the highest rating in at least two of the following books that are available to you at your public library:

Best's Insurance Reports
Standard & Poor's
Moody's

Duff & Phelps
Weiss Research, Inc.

If you are new to an area and do not know anyone to ask, look in the yellow pages of your phone book. Agencies representing various insurance companies are listed there. Call several agencies, find out which companies they represent, and then check the rating of the companies in the above publications. Then call back and ask for an agent who has one of the following designations, depending on the type insurance you need. (The CLU or a CPCU designation does not always mean these people are superior agents, but it does mean they have done additional study.)

- CLU (Certified Life Underwriter) is the health and life insurance agent's most distinctive designation for agent licenses.
- CPCU (Chartered Property and Casualty Underwriter) is the automobile and homeowner's insurance agent's highest designation for agent licensing.

An agent who works full-time will give your case more study than part-time and marginal agents. Be sure that the agent is willing to take time to find out your specific needs and goals for your future and the future of your family. Do not rely on your agent to sell you the right policy. Be informed so that you can make the right decision for the coverage you need, then read the policy carefully when you get it. (Information regarding various types of insurance—health, homeowner's, auto, and life—are included in chapter 10, "Protecting Your Assets.")

Your agent should be able to offer you policies from several different companies, not just one. Rates are different with each company, and you want to be able to compare policies and companies in order to select the one that is right for your situation.

Your agent should not try to sell you more coverage than you need or can afford. One should never carry more than one policy with the same coverage. Double coverage is not allowed by most insurance companies. If you feel that you are being pressured to buy a policy you don't need, change agents.

If an agent encourages you to "buy the policy now because you may not be able to get insurance later," ask for a complete explanation. If you are not satisfied, find another agent.

How an Agent Is Paid

Insurance agents work on commissions. When one sells you a policy, a commission is earned from the insurance company that issued the policy. If you renew it, additional commissions can be earned, depending on the insurance company. For every additional policy an agent sells you, a commission is earned. If you convert a lower-premium policy to a higher-premium policy, a commission is earned.

Insurance agents may be able to work on a fee basis if they have the appropriate license. As an example, if you need an agent to review the policies that another agent has sold you and to make recommendations, he could work on an hourly fee, since he would not expect to receive a commission by selling you a policy.

10

Protecting Your Assets

MONEY

It was the first night of one of our courses at the local college. A good friend, Arlene, had enrolled in the course, and she approached us a couple of minutes before we were to begin.

"Barb and Donnette, I just thought you ought to know this. Ann, seated behind me, is a neighbor of mine—her husband just died two weeks ago. You'll never believe this, because she's a high school English teacher and certainly well educated and articulate—but she has never paid a bill or balanced a checkbook. She's just lost and doesn't know where to turn first."

"Oh, yes, we do believe it. Women are not as sheltered by their husbands as they used to be, but it certainly still happens," we assured Arlene. We kept Ann in mind as we began our session of "Protecting Your Assets."

Checking Accounts

Most women today are knowledgeable about maintaining a checkbook—paying bills on time and balancing the checkbook each month. If you are not, all banks are delighted to assist you in opening a checking account, and most banks are happy to give you information as to how to maintain a checking account.

A ledger is provided for listing all deposits and checks written. A statement arrives regularly (usually monthly) from the bank, at which time you reconcile your checkbook with the bank's statement. Do this within two to three days of receiving your statement. Banks—and bank's computers—make mistakes, too, and the sooner within the time of receiving your statement you reconcile your checkbook, the sooner you can clear up any errors—whether they are yours or the bank's.

In shopping for a checking account, be aware that there are various types: regular checking accounts, interest-bearing checking accounts, and money market checking accounts. Make sure that the institution provides that your account is federally insured up to $100,000.

Regular checking accounts are numerous and there is healthy competition among them. They want you for a customer! These accounts allow an unlimited number of checks to be written each month, and if you maintain the institution's required minimum balance, you will not be charged a service charge. Shop around for the lowest required minimum balance. Note that some checking accounts may have a very low minimum balance requirement and do not charge a service charge; however, they may not return your checks in your statement each month. Instead, you may be furnished only with a monthly computer printout of your check transactions and may receive the actual check upon request (within a few days and sometimes for a fee). If it is important to you that your checks be returned with the statement, be sure to read the small print of the agreement carefully.

Interest-bearing checking accounts require you to maintain a minimum balance (usually $500 to $2500). You may write unlimited checks, and you will be paid a low interest on the amount of the balance you maintain. If your balance falls below the required minimum, there is usually a service charge for that month.

Money market checking accounts allow only three to five checks to be written on the account each month; however, interest rates paid are higher than regular interest-bearing checking accounts, competing with money market mutual funds. The difference is that these bank accounts are usually federally insured up to $100,000 and money market mutual funds at brokerage houses are not. You may withdraw any amount you wish from money market checking accounts; however, if your balance slips below the required minimum, it will pay lower rates. Some banks provide that if you have both a regular checking account and a money market checking account, you may designate that should you overdraw the regular checking account it may be taken automatically from the money market account. There is a limitation on how often you may overdraw, of course!

If you are computer literate, you can make your bookkeeping much easier, and a lot more fun. Even if you're not a computer whiz, it's easy to learn. Call your local community college and ask when the next computer course on such bookkeeping software as "Quicken" or "Managing Your Money" is offered. These are but two of the easy-to-learn computer software packages for keeping your books in order. You can maintain all your bookkeeping, designate budget categories, and indicate tax-deductible contributions all at the same time you're entering the checks into the computer. Then, at tax time, you're all prepared, with categories indicated for every check you've written.

Your Credit Rating

To maintain a good credit rating, you must pay your bills on time. Sounds simple, doesn't it? The whole secret, of course, is living within your means and not buying more than you can afford. But the time usually comes for all of us when we must borrow money—perhaps for a car, a home, to start a new business, or to help put the kids through college. And to borrow money, we need to have a good credit history. The best idea is to establish a good credit history *before* you really need it. Here's how it goes:

Jack and Karen married two years before they graduated from law school. They had about $2,700 left in their savings account when they graduated, and had not yet established a line of credit. Karen and Jack withdrew $1,500 of the $2,700, then deposited it in a savings account at the bank from which they wanted to obtain the loan. Using the $1,500 as collateral, they obtained the loan to buy a piece of furniture, then repaid the loan in a timely manner. Bingo! Jack and Karen had established a credit history. (Note: Be sure that the period of the loan is for at least a year, so that it will appear on your credit rating. The banks call these loans "rated loans.") Some banks are reluctant to make loans just so the borrower can establish a credit history, so do not mention this at the time you're applying.

BARBARA: *Soon after I filed for divorce, my attorney advised me to establish a credit history immediately in my legal name, Barbara Tom Jowell. My married name, Mrs. W. H. Jowell, had been only a social name, explained the lawyer, and all women need to establish credit in their legal names.*

My experience was similar to Karen and Jack's. I purchased a CD [certificate of deposit] at a bank to use as collateral for a loan. I borrowed the money—for only 1 percent over prime because of having such good collateral. After paying off the loan, I had established a credit history in my own name, Barbara Tom Jowell. I had also established a line of credit with that bank, so that any time in the future I should need a quick loan of money (up to a certain amount), I could immediately be granted that loan.

Criteria for Credit

Whether you're seeking a loan from a bank, securing a mortgage for a house, or applying for credit from a credit card company, similar criteria are used for granting your credit wishes:

- Your type of employment and type of income (amount and how paid—monthly, weekly, by commission, etc.).
- Your nonemployment income (investments, interest, royalties, or other sources of income).

- Your assets (Do you own your home, other real estate, savings accounts, stocks, bonds, mutual funds, managed accounts, limited partnerships, gold coins?)
- Your debts and your credit history (What do you owe? Do you pay your debts on time? Have you ever declared bankruptcy?)
- Your expenses (number of children, other dependents, standard of living—such as club memberships, number of automobiles).

Credit Cards

As we've mentioned elsewhere in this book, if you are widowed and your credit cards are all in your late husband's name, you may wish to wait awhile before advising the credit card companies of his death. The credit card companies may force you to reapply, and if your household income is substantially lower because of losing his income, your credit limits will be much lower.

DONNETTE: *I kept the joint credit cards, paid the charges in full each month, then reapplied in my legal name two years later, insisting on the same limits because of my excellent credit history. The credit card companies granted my requests.*

If a woman finds herself suddenly single, without any credit in her own name, she may have to wait until she establishes some sort of credit history before a credit card company will grant her a card. To the best of her ability, she should pay bills— rent, utility, "inherited debts"—as expeditiously as possible. If you find that you will have trouble paying a debt, contact the creditor immediately and explain your situation. Even if you pay only a few dollars a week, most creditors will work with you if they know you are sincere in your efforts to pay the debt.

Taking Care of Your Credit

Once you've attained a good credit rating, take care of it. Here are a few tips:

Pay the full balance of your credit cards monthly. If you can't do this immediately, shop around until you locate a credit card with the lowest interest rate available and no annual fee. Then transfer all your debt to that credit card and systematically pay off the entire debt. Or, if you have a savings account, use a portion of your savings to pay off your credit card. You're no doubt getting far less interest off that savings account than you're paying in interest on that credit card. Then exercise your willpower. Don't charge more than you can pay for—in full—monthly.

Order a copy of your credit history to see that all is correct. Listed under "Credit Reporting Agencies" in the yellow pages of your telephone book are the agencies that will furnish a copy of your credit history. Call one of the agencies and order one. There is a small charge unless you have been turned down for credit, in which case it is free of charge. If there is any incorrect information on your report, call to ask the agency's procedure to have it removed. Even if they have you listed for a credit card you do not have (perhaps you received the card unsolicited through the mail, cut it up, and threw it away), be sure to advise the agency of this. Strangely enough, having too many credit cards could be a detriment in applying for a loan, as this reflects how much credit you *have access to,* and could conceivably take advantage of, thus overextending yourself.

Keep a copy of all your credit cards—front and back. Leave the list with a trusted friend or in a safe-deposit box when you leave home, in case your wallet is stolen. An easy method is to photocopy both sides of your cards.

INVESTMENTS

We need to seek investments to help us realize the varying financial goals during our lifetime. In our youth we may be investing for a down payment on our first home, later on we need funds for family vacations and to send the children to college, and finally we plan for retirement.

John H. Alpers, CFP, managing director, Gateway Financial

Strategies, LLC, of Boulder, Colorado, advises that every port-folio should contain assets in four categories: cash and equiv-alents, equities such as stocks and stock mutual funds, debt such as bonds, and real assets. The percentage allocated to each of these categories will be the major determining factor in the level of risk and expected rate of return on your overall portfolio. The percentage of assets allocated to each of the above categories must be adjusted to changes in your own personal circum-stances, such as a career change or a change of risk tolerance, as well as changes in the general economic climate.

Categories of Investments

Cash and cash equivalents. This category includes cash in your checking and savings accounts, money market accounts, short-term CDs (certificates of deposit), and T-bills (treasury bills). You need enough cash or cash equivalents for (a) emergen-cies and (b) to allow you to take advantage of a good investment opportunity.

Equities (stocks, stock mutual funds). With this investment, you own shares in a company (or the mutual fund in which you invest owns shares in various companies). On a long-term basis, equities have historically provided superior overall total return in the form of capital growth and dividends. They also provide some inflation growth and dividends, as well as some inflation protection. The degree of risk can vary greatly. For example, "blue-chip" stocks are generally considered to be low-risk invest-ments, while "penny stocks" are considered to be extremely risky. Diversification and continuous portfolio supervision are the keys to success in this challenging arena.

Debt instruments (bonds and bond mutual funds). These are assets in which the investor is the lender of the funds invested. The primary advantages of debt-based assets are that they usually have a fairly low degree of risk if held to maturity, carry a guaranteed rate of return, and are generally liquid. Since bonds generally have a fixed rate of return, they can turn out to be poor investments during periods of high inflation. A bond yielding 9 percent is not a very appealing investment if interest rates rise and new bonds are paying 12 percent. The reverse also holds true. During times of falling interest rates or deflation, a bond yielding 9 percent will look pretty good when compared to new bonds yielding 6 percent. Despite their drawbacks, it is prudent to maintain a portion of your assets in bonds to provide balance and liquidity to your portfolio.

Real assets. These are assets which are tangible, that we can actually "touch," such as real estate, antiques, jewelry, and oil and gas. Real assets may provide income or tax savings or both (such as in rental property). The location of the property, the financial structure of the transaction, and the management of the property are the keys to its financial performance. Although a home is not primarily an investment asset, the equity you've acquired in your home may satisfy the percentage requirements of this investment category.

Alpers points out that the single most important variable in investment performance, other than asset allocation, is your own personal time frame for results. Be patient. Choose an investment strategy and stick with it. More time allows for greater volatility in your portfolio, but by the same token the passage of time allows for the smoothing out of the investment curve.

Higher volatility and risk are associated with the stock market, but the stock market provides the best returns over time.

SURVIVAL TIP

One of the best ways to begin to assemble an investment portfolio is within the retirement or pension plan offered by your employer. Here, investments may be tax deferred and/or matched to some degree by the employer.

If you are self-employed or your employer does not offer a retirement or pension plan, you must do your own planning for retirement. Consult a financial planner.

Annuities

There are two types of annuities: immediate annuities and de-ferred annuities. Retirees or soon-to-be retirees often use imme-diate annuities as an investment vehicle, depositing a lump sum with an insurance company or other financial entity to be invested in a guaranteed-income account. The company guaran-tees to make payments back to the client for the period of their lifetime. A certain amount of each payment back is not taxable, because that portion is categorized as being a return of their principal.

With a deferred annuity, you deposit a sum of money to be invested, then draw upon it in the future, say, upon retirement. No taxes are paid on the investment earnings until you begin to withdraw them from the annuity. With a fixed deferred annuity, you will receive a fixed amount as a monthly payment, for lifetime or another guaranteed period of time. If you die earlier than the fixed period, your beneficiary will receive payments for the remainder of that period of time, which is usually ten, fifteen, or twenty years.

With a variable deferred annuity, you can choose to invest some of your funds in a choice of mutual funds as well as a guaranteed income account, giving you the chance that your payments might increase if the funds perform well.

Research carefully the strength of the company from whom you purchase fixed annuities. Buy only from those companies rated A+ by Best's Insurance Reports. (Check your local library.)

As you assemble a portfolio of investments, remind yourself, "No one is responsible for me but me. I must keep my business in order. I must understand what I am investing in." Subscribe to a personal finance magazine, such as *Money* or *Smart Money*. If you are considering a mutual fund investment, read the pros-pectus carefully. Then go to your public library and check the *Morningstar* rating of the mutual fund. *Morningstar* uses a simple star system to rate mutual funds, with five stars being the highest rating and one the lowest. In order to determine the appropriate number of stars, *Morningstar* considers how well a fund has balanced risk and return in the past. It is best to consider funds that have done well over five to ten years, rather than just recent performance.

For guidance in attaining your goals, seek the advice of professionals *after* you have familiarized yourself with different types of investments. For instance, a financial planner can help you identify your goals and investment risk tolerance and then give you guidance as to what types of investments can attain those goals. There are fee-only, commission-only, and combination fee-and-commission financial planners. The fee-only planner can give you direction but cannot sell you any investments, in which case you would turn to a stockbroker to implement the financial adviser's suggestions. Commission-only planners and combination commission-and-fee planners can also sell investments. A tax accountant or tax attorney could give you advice as to how to minimize taxes, and an estate attorney would give you advice about structuring your will most advantageously for yourself and your heirs. Insurance agents will give you guidance on your insurance needs. Chapter 9, "The Professionals You Work With: Who, What, When, Where, and How," gives you information on choosing and interviewing advisers.

Finally, keep reminding yourself, "I must stay aware of how my investments are doing."

• Quarterly (four times a year), you will need to look at the growth or loss of the various categories of investments and then reallocate the investments in your portfolio to meet your goals. Every three months, make an appointment with your financial planner or stockbroker, both for self-education and for the purpose of any necessary reallocating of investments in your portfolio.

SURVIVAL TIP

Remember to take into account the assets in your pension fund as you are considering the big picture of your portfolio and your investment goals.

RETIREMENT PLANNING

If you have not started planning for retirement, start today. Social security benefits were never intended to provide totally for the retirement years of America! Americans are living longer than ever before. Without some prudent investing for our future, we could find ourselves living far more modestly than we would want, even though we may have pension plans. In contemplating your retirement, consider the following:

* At what age do you plan to retire?
* What will your income be? Factor in how much income you will receive from social security, pension plans, and investments. Do you plan to work part-time?
* Formulate a retirement budget, taking into account your lifestyle, travel plans, debts, rent or mortgage and tax payments, and special health care costs.
* Also consider whether there's a certain sum of money you wish to pass on to your children. A general rule of thumb is that in retirement you will probably need about 75 to 80 percent of an average of the last five years of your annual employment income, assuming that your home is paid for and your children are finished with their education. If your home is not paid for or you still have children to send through college, you will probably need to continue earning the same annual income that you had over the last five years. To reach either of these goals, you need to start early in life making prudent investments to support you in your retirement years.
* If you have a substantial estate, you will need to do prudent estate tax planning, structuring your will to take advantage of methods to minimize taxes. Perhaps you will wish to take advantage of a law allowing you to give up to $10,000 a year to anyone without having to pay gift taxes. You could invest $10,000 in a mutual fund in a beneficiary's name. You may want to buy life insurance to pay estate taxes. *See a certified financial planner!*

LIFE INSURANCE

Do you really need life insurance? If you are a single woman with no dependents, beware of buying more life insurance than you really need. Perhaps you need only enough coverage to provide for your debts and burial expenses.

There are nearly 2,500 companies selling life insurance, and choosing the best policy for this time in life can be confusing. Using our tips for selecting advisers (See chapter 9, "The Professionals You Work With"), choose someone with whom you feel comfortable, who is well respected with excellent credentials, and who has been in the business for at least five years.

Term Insurance

Term insurance gives you life insurance coverage for a definite period of time—usually from five to twenty years. The premium or cost of the insurance purchases risk coverage after the expenses are deducted from the premium. Premiums for term life insurance usually increase periodically as you become older; however, the annual premium for term insurance is much lower initially than the premium for comparable whole life insurance purchased at the same time.

Be aware that:

• Some term policies mandate that you undergo medical requalification every four, five, or ten years to keep your premiums at the lower term levels.
• Term insurance premiums do increase as you get older.
• Once you are over fifty-five, it is expensive to acquire this kind of insurance.

Who should buy term insurance? People who need protection for specific goals—for instance, to cover the house mortgage or college tuition for children and cannot afford whole life insurance.

Whole Life Insurance

Whole life, or ordinary life insurance, covers you for your "whole" or entire life and offers a guaranteed amount payable to your beneficiary when you die. Some whole life policies pay dividends. These dividends can:

- Reduce your premiums.
- Buy paid-up additions to your life insurance policy, which would increase your death benefit.
- Be given back to you in cash, or be left on deposit with the insurance company, where they will earn interest and serve as a type of savings account.

When you buy a whole life policy, part of the premium pays the cost of the insurance risk, part pays the insurer's expenses, and part goes into a reserve fund that is known as the "cash value fund." The cash value, which allows the premiums to remain level during your lifetime, builds up annually and grows in value on a tax-deferred basis.

If the owner of the policy decides to stop paying the premiums, she can terminate the policy and take the built-up cash values, minus any potential surrender charge. Other options include the purchase of a paid-up policy with a reduced death benefit, or a term policy with an equal death benefit but for a limited number of years. The number of years of coverage will depend on the insured's age and amount of cash values available.

A newer variation of the whole life contract is called second-to-die, which insures two lives, and pays the death benefit when the second person dies. The cost of a second-to-die policy is lower than two individual policies. This is sometimes used by a couple with a large estate to pay estate taxes when the second spouse dies.

Be aware that:

- The premiums for whole life insurance are higher than term life because some money goes toward the cash value.
- Not all whole life policies pay dividends. Even when dividends are paid, they reflect the insurance company's earnings after expenses and are not guaranteed.

Who should buy whole life insurance? This policy is well suited to people whose needs do not diminish over time, for example, someone who intends for the death benefits to be used to pay his/her estate taxes.

Variations of Whole Life Insurance

Universal life insurance. The actual insurance cost and cash values are more flexible. The premium is used first to pay for insurance protection and expenses. Any excess money is held by the insurance company at a rate of interest which is predetermined annually. The minimum rate (3.5 to 4 percent right now) is guaranteed by the contract; however, it is the current rate that is in fact credited to your account.

Be aware that:

- The investment return on your cash value is tied to interest rates. When rates are high, universal life looks more attractive. When the interest rates are low, whole life looks more attractive.
- Although you are allowed flexibility in determining the premium you pay each year, you need a lot of willpower to set aside enough for premium payments each year. If you fail to pay enough premium, your death benefit will not be as large, or you will have to come up with bigger premium payments later on to make up the difference. This flexibility allows (within certain guidelines) the policy owner to modify the policy face amount or premium in response to changing needs and circumstances.

Who should buy universal life insurance? The answer is the same as for whole life, but it is best for people who want to see how their premiums are used and want flexibility in how they pay their premiums—for example, someone with ever-changing business, financial, and family circumstances.

Variable life insurance. The rate of return of the cash value is not determined by the insurance company. Instead, it is dependent on the earnings of mutual funds within the contract selected by the insured. Mutual funds offered range from very conservative to very aggressive.

Be aware that:

There are fixed premium payments and a guaranteed death benefit; however, there is no guaranteed cash value, because you take on the investment risk yourself, and could wind up with little or no cash value if the stock/bond markets decline.

Who should buy variable life insurance? Those who are risk tolerant and enjoy stock/bond market investing.

HEALTH INSURANCE

Most Americans get their health insurance through group plans with their employers or through an organization. Be sure you understand the preexisting condition clause and what period of time it covers. (A preexisting condition clause specifies that you will not be not be covered for specific health problems you or your family had before the policy became effective. The preexisting condition clause can be for various lengths of time.)

A case in point, here:

DONNETTE: *My late husband, Mac, had his first bypass surgery at the age of thirty-six and was covered by his employer's health plan. Two years later Mac went into business for himself and searched for health insurance, but was unable to get coverage for heart disease, as it had been a "preexisting condition." Mac and I had to pay for the second bypass surgery ourselves.*

- What is the maximum coverage of your major medical policy? Is it for each illness, or for one year, or over your lifetime? Is it for each member of the family, or for the family as a whole? You need to look for a policy with at least $1 million in maximum coverage, in order to cover a major illness.
- What is the deductible amount you must pay before the coverage starts? Is it for the family as a whole or for each family member? Is it based on each new claim, or on an annual basis, no matter how many claims you make that year?
- What is the dependent coverage? Some policies cover all children, including those away at school or not living at home. Some restrict coverage to a specific age.
- What is excluded? Maternity benefits? Nursing home care? Dental? Prescriptions? Cosmetic surgery? Substance abuse treatment? Psychotherapy?

- Are you required to get a second opinion before surgery?
- Are you required to get hospital preadmission authorization and presurgery review in order to get regular benefits?
- If you leave your job, can you convert your group plan to an individual policy?
- Are you aware of the COBRA act? This act requires employers to inform their employees that they are eligible for health coverage under the company's health plan for up to eighteen months after they have left employment for any reason, either resignation or dismissal. The employee is responsible for the premiums. Also under COBRA, a divorced or widowed woman and her dependents are eligible for health coverage under her former spouse's health plan for up to thirty-six months. Here again, she is responsible for the premiums.
- What are the cancellation provisions of the policy? Some policies are noncancelable, regardless of what your health is; some are limited to a specific period of time, such as two or three years.
- Is the policy guaranteed renewable? If so, the insurance company is obligated to renew the policy. They can, however, change the premium.

SURVIVAL TIP

If you have trouble getting insurance because of a preexisting condition such as cancer or heart problems, call the National Underwriter Company, which has published a book, *Who Writes What in Life and Health Insurance,* at (513) 721-2140. If you're looking for additional information about health insurance, order the brochure *What You Should Know About Health Insurance,* which is published by the Health Insurance Association of America (HIAA), at (202) 824-1600.

DISABILITY INSURANCE

If you become unable to work, unable to take care of yourself and the family that depends on you, how would you manage? If you've planned to work to a ripe old age and a devastating illness or accident cuts you down, you may find your income diminishes as your expenses rise.

Disability coverage replaces lost income if you are incapacitated. If your employer provides disability insurance, you're one of the lucky few. Most people who have disability coverage purchase a private plan.

According to the U.S. government's *Commissioners Standard Ordinary Mortality and Disabilities Tables,* if you are now age 35, you have a one in five chance of becoming temporarily or permanently disabled over the next fifteen years, compared to a one in fifteen chance of dying.

Social security coverage includes limited disability coverage. If the disability you suffer is expected to last for at least a year and you will be unable to work at any job during that time, your social security disability benefits will begin after six months. However, during the first six months, you may be totally without income. Knowing that makes purchasing a disability policy attractive.

There are three factors to consider in such a policy:

1. How long is the waiting period before the policy pays benefits?
2. How long will the insurance company continue to pay benefits?
3. How is disability defined?

To keep an individual policy affordable, increase the period you must wait before the insurance company starts sending monthly checks. Can you hold out until your sick pay stops? Check your policy at work. If you have enough savings to live for six months without pay, choose the policy that doesn't kick in for six months.

Be sure that your policy covers you until you're sixty-five years old and your social security will cover the disability. Even then, you may want to buy a bigger disability policy if you think you cannot live on the amount you will receive from social security. However, the more coverage you will receive, the more expensive the policy will be.

Be sure that the definition of "disability" in the policy includes coverage if you decide to work in a less demanding job that pays less money.

LONG-TERM CARE INSURANCE

Long-term care is the kind of help you need if you are unable to care for yourself because of a lengthy illness or disability. It refers to care provided in a nursing home, at home, or in the community. It can range from help with routine daily activities like eating or dressing to twenty-four-hour care by skilled medical personnel.

The cost of long-term care is expensive. Today, the national average cost of nursing home care is at least $30,000 a year; home care averages $10,000 to $15,000 a year. These figures will probably double in twenty years. These high costs can exhaust your savings in a very short time. Where will the money come from if you need these services at some time in the future?

You can use your own resources. In this case, you have the income and assets to pay for long-term care without seriously affecting your financial well-being or your independence.

You can qualify for government assistance. If you meet federal and/or state poverty levels for both income and assets, your state will pay your long-term care bills through Medicaid. But choices for the care you receive may be limited. Furthermore, if you do qualify for state aid on the basis of impoverishment (having few if any financial assets *or* having successfully *shifted* your financial assets to someone else so as to qualify), several states have recently enacted legislation to place liens on the homes of Medicaid recipients. After your death (and the death of your spouse, if later), up to 100 percent of the equity in your home will be used to pay back the state for the taxpayers' cost for your long-term care.

You can be insured. Long-term care insurance can help you protect your assets and your independence. *It should be noted:* While the premium cost of long-term care insurance remains level once you are enrolled, your age at that point is the driving factor in the premium amount. The cost of the premium goes up at a geometric rate, the longer you wait to become enrolled.

The right policy provides:

- Guaranteed renewability.
- Nursing home and home health care.
- Payment triggered by the policyholder's inability to perform at least two of five basic activities of daily living (bathing, feeding, administering medications, toileting, and transferring from chair to a bed).
- Coverage in the event you develop Alzheimer's disease.

Before buying a policy

- Consider the term of the policy. If you are under age sixty, lifetime coverage is preferable. If you are over age eighty, opt for two or four years. Those people between the ages of sixty and eighty should buy what they can afford.
- Consider the policy's elimination (waiting) period. The longer the elimination period, the lower the premium. The elimination period is the period between the commencement of your disability and the time benefits actually begin. Consider the trade-off between price and peace of mind. For most people, a 100-day elimination period may make the most sense because, if they are eligible, Medicare may pay some of the expenses for the first 100 days.

HOMEOWNER'S INSURANCE

Be sure you know whether you are buying replacement cost or depreciated (actual value) cost insurance for both home and personal property.

Be sure to take note of what is excluded. You may want to buy additional coverage for one or more of your exclusions (which commonly include earthquakes, floods, mud slides).

Check how much your jewelry, furs, cash, silverware, and collections are insured for under your regular homeowner's policy. Most policies place a total limitation of five hundred dollars on the combined worth of all those valuables, plus other restrictions—such as the place of the loss. You can insure any specific items you choose at their replacement (or depreciated) value by adding an endorsement to your policy or buying a separate personal property floater that covers you wherever the loss occurs.

DONNETTE: *For instance, my wedding ring is insured for replacement cost no matter where or how I lose it—even washing my hands in a restaurant's ladies' room.*

Keep household inventory records in your safe-deposit box. Pictures are good reminders of details.

Do you have individually valuable items? If not, but you feel that your general furnishings are worth more than the 50 percent your homeowner's policy automatically covers them for, you can increase that personal property coverage up to 70 percent of your home's stated value.

Do you have a pool house or guest house or cabana? If so, check your policy's coverage for "other structures." Most policies insure them for 10 percent of your home's value. If they are worth more than that amount, increase that coverage in your policy.

Ask your agent about an automatic inflation-protection clause in your policy. If you elect to get an automatic inflation-protection clause, check the insured value of your home each year. (The automatic inflation-protection clause can result in overinsuring your home if you are not careful.) Review your policy periodically, and adjust for home improvements, changing property values, and (as mentioned above) inflation.

Don't gamble what you can't afford to lose. A deductible of $2,500 may be affordable, but $10,000 may not be. If you are renting, you need renter's insurance.

If you have a great deal of property to protect and liability awards are relatively high in your state, you may want to consider purchasing an umbrella policy to cover your assets. It will cover your expenses if you are charged with libel, slander, or invasion of privacy, or injuring someone and the judgment goes against you. Without this kind of coverage, the amount levied against you must be satisfied out of your own assets, which may bankrupt you.

AUTOMOBILE INSURANCE

As a widow or a single person, you might consider dropping comprehensive and/or collision coverage on an older vehicle. By the time a car is six or seven years old, it has lost most of its original value and your insurance company is going to pay only the actual market value of your car if it is wrecked in a collision. However, before you make this decision, discuss the subject with your automobile insurance agent to make sure you feel comfortable with your decision.

Our friend had a seven-year-old car that was wrecked in a collision. Her insurance adjuster looked up the car's worth in the Blue Book. Since the Blue Book showed the car's value at $2,000, that was the maximum the insurance company could pay her for the car. *The insurance company pays only the actual cash value.* It is not a replacement policy. To have the car repaired was going to cost $4,000! However, in this case, after the initial shock wore off, our friend was glad she was able to get even $2,000 so she could at least replace her car with one that cost $2,000. Discuss this thoroughly with your agent to see how much risk you are willing to assume.

Coverage You Need

Liability:

* *Bodily injury.* Covers damage to other people.
* *Property damage.* Covers damage to other people's property.

Comprehensive:

* Covers damage to your car by fire, theft, vandalism, hail, glass breakage, etc.
* Covers damage to your car by collision with a car or object.

Other Forms of Coverage

Some of the following may be covered by other policies or included in your main policy. If so, you do not need duplicate coverage.

- *No-fault.* Covers medical, funeral expenses, lost wages and other basic auto insurance.
- *Medical payments.* Covers medical and funeral expenses.
- *Emergency road service.* Covers towing and roadside service.
- *Car rental expense.* Covers rental car if yours is damaged.

- *Death/dismemberment.* Covers death or certain combinations of injuries.
- *Specialty coverage.* Covers audio equipment, glass breakage, etc.

In some states, some coverages are required. Check your state rules through your agent.

cost of insurance is minimal, and you will save a good bit of money should you ever own a "lemon"—or your car has unsolved problems.

WILLS

We urge our seminar participants, "If you don't have a will, and if you don't do another thing as a result of this seminar, please, please get an up-to-date will."

Your will is your way of distributing your estate the way you want it done. Why should you let this all-important resolution of your life's possessions be left to someone else, or worse, to an impersonal officer of the court?

Types of Wills

- A *formal will* is written by an attorney and witnessed as to the laws required by the state where you live.
- A *statutory will* is written on a form with wording that has been approved by your state, also witnessed as to the laws required by the state where you live.
- A *holographic will* is composed by you in your writing. It is not witnessed, but you do have to sign and date it. Because lay terminology can be so ambiguous, we do not recommend a holographic will. (Also, some states do not recognize holographic wills.)

Some of your assets do not have to go through a will and thus avoid probate:

- Assets placed in a trust.
- Assets held in joint tenancy.
- Proceeds from life insurance policy. These go directly to the beneficiary—unless the beneficiary is the estate.
- Retirement plan benefits in cases where you may name a beneficiary to receive the balance remaining in the account at the time of the owner's death.

You should always name alternate beneficiaries in case the primary beneficiaries die before you do.

If your estate is large enough to be subject to estate or inheritance taxes, those taxes have to be paid before the beneficiaries of your will receive the property. If you are leaving a sizable estate, you may consider getting extra life insurance to pay the taxes.

Choose your executor carefully, and ask his or her permission to be named as executor. You may want to choose a close friend who is financially savvy or a trust department of a bank. You may decide it would be prudent to have coexecutors. Executor's fees are usually determined by the state, but it is sometimes possible to decide upon those fees prior to your death. It often causes problems between siblings to choose one child over another. Remember to choose an alternate executor in case your executor dies before you.

You may choose to place assets in trust, as mentioned above. Choose someone skilled at handling money, as the trustee's primary duty is to make investments for your heirs. Every state has laws governing trustees, but their fees usually are not governed by law. You may set trustees' fees ahead of time, or fees may be set by the court. Be sure to choose an alternate trustee.

Common Types of Trusts

Testamentary trusts. This type of trust is designated in your will, which means your estate must be probated before the assets can be placed into the trust. Its primary use is to manage the inheritance for heirs who are not financially experienced enough to do so for themselves.

A testamentary trust may also be a tax-saving device, the most common being the A-B Trust. Federal law states that a spouse may inherit an unlimited amount; however, assets left to other heirs are not unlimited. Check with your tax professional for the nearest changes in the tax law.

Living (inter vivos) trusts. Assets within a living trust do not have to pass through the probate process. A living trust takes effect during your lifetime and lasts for a specified length of time. It may be revocable or irrevocable. With a revocable living trust, you maintain control and may change it at any time; however, the property within a revocable living trust will be subject to estate and inheritance taxes. In an irrevocable trust you relinquish all control of the assets and provisions of the trust, which can run permanently or for a designated period of time. Although some irrevocable trusts provide that portions of the estate are removed from the estate and are consequently not taxed upon your death, you may feel uncomfortable knowing you may never change the provisions during the lifetime of the trust.

In all cases, you must seek qualified legal advice when establishing trusts.

Living Wills

Each state has its own requirements for living wills. To obtain a sample living will to use as a guideline, write: Concern for Dying, 250 West 57 Street, New York, NY 10017. Check with your attorney as to the specific requirements of the state in which you live.

Durable Power of Attorney

A durable power of attorney designates the person who would handle your financial and business decisions if you are incapacitated and unable to do so. Your attorney will assist you in executing a durable power of attorney.

Durable Power of Attorney for Health Care

A durable power of attorney for health care designates the person who will make decisions regarding your health care if you are incapacitated and unable to do so. Your attorney will assist you in executing a durable power of attorney for health care.

11

Buying or Selling a Home

SELLING THE HOME

"All night long, the house seems to creak and complain. Every little noise wakes me up, then I lie there and think about what I should do. Sometimes I think I'll be so glad to get out of this house, and then I turn around and get all emotional about the thought of leaving. We had a lot of good years here—but honestly, the location's not as good as it used to be, and I know if I'm going to stay here I ought to redo it from top to bottom, paint it, or something. The thought of putting the house on the market is enough to send me over the edge."

Brooks Thurman is alone, for the first time in her life. First she was her daddy's little girl, then she got married, and now it's just her, rattling around in that big old house. There are some days when her home is the only place she feels safe—and other days when the house itself seems to be the source of all her problems.

One of the first decisions a woman alone must make is about the house, at a time when she is mentally and physically exhausted. To help you organize your thoughts, we suggest you sit down with a pad and pencil and begin to formulate answers to three questions.

Questions to Ask Yourself

You might not know all the answers right now. After you've read this chapter, do some soul-searching and number crunching. Then come back to the questions in two weeks after you have done your homework and have carefully considered the issues.

If you are newly widowed or divorced, and unless you are in financial difficulty, do not make any major decisions, such as selling the family home, for a year. In a year, come back to these questions:

- Do I really want to keep the house? Do I have sufficient time and help to maintain it? Would (or could) I be happier elsewhere?
- Can I afford to keep the house? Consider not only the mortgage payments but the taxes and maintenance as well.
- Can I afford to sell the house? At first glance, this appears to be a strange question; however, you must consider the capital gains tax on the sale of your home, as well as the realtor's commission and legal fees. In the past, the cost of capital gains taxes were often a big concern to home sellers. As of August 1997, new capital gains tax laws allowing substantial tax-free exclusion on home sale profits came into effect. Now there is a $250,000 tax-free exclusion for singles and a $500,000 exclusion for couples filing jointly. The law requiring one to be fifty-five or older to gain an exclusion has been abolished. Now, most home sellers will not be obliged to pay capital gains taxes when they sell, regardless of their age.

The home must have been your principal residence for two out of five years, so the exclusion nay be used as often as every two years, if necessary. In many cases, a person who must relocate suddenly because of a job change, health reasons, or other unforeseen circumstances—without having met the two-year requirement—may still exclude a portion of the $250,000 or $500,000 amount. The excluded gain would be equal to the fraction of time the home has been one's principal residence. For instance, if one had to relocate after living in the house for only one year, one could possibly claim one-half of the exclusion. Consult your tax professional for details about your situation.

Choosing a Realtor

If your decision is to sell, we strongly recommend using a real estate agent or broker, at a cost of approximately 6 percent of the selling price of the house. (The 6 percent brokerage fee is sometimes negotiable, so try to bargain for a lesser fee.) If the agent's fee sounds high, ask yourself if *you* are willing to do the following:

- Do the research to set the asking price. This includes an analysis of properties recently sold in your neighborhood, as well as those on the market now.
- Handle all the advertising.
- Secure an appraisal and get home inspectors.
- Stay aware of financing. Local mortgage lenders can give you current fees, but interest rates are subject to change daily.
- Show the house, perhaps frequently being alone in the house with the shopper.
- When you do get an offer, be able to negotiate the offer if it is not acceptable, qualify the buyer (ascertain if they can get a loan), and prepare a sales agreement, to name a few details.
- When the contract is signed, then coordinate inspectors, surveyors, attorneys, and loan officers in order to facilitate a successful closing.

Here are some tips on how to choose the right realtor:

- Ask friends, neighbors, and colleagues for their recommendations.
- Seek an experienced, full-time agent, one that specializes in your type of property.
- Try to choose an agency that is a member of a multiple-listing service, thus giving your home maximum exposure to the market.
- Ask how your home will be marketed. Ask for a sample advertisement of your home. Ask if the agent will hold an open house to launch your property.

- Be sure the length of the contract is the standard three to six months. Ask for progress reports to be given to you periodically, say every three weeks. If your agent does not generate substantial exposure for your home, find another agent for the next listing period.
- If you have any possible prospects to buy your home directly from you, make sure that you can list those persons as exceptions in the agreement with the agent.
- Interview several agents. Ask for references and check them.
- Make sure the agent will be easily accessible to you, and that you feel comfortable and secure with him or her.
- Beware of any agent who suggests an unusually high selling price. This may be a ruse to get you to list with him or her, then you may later be talked into reducing the sales price.

Tips Toward a Quick Sale

Get a warranty. Warranty insurance will insure (less a standard deductible) against mechanical failures and breakdown from normal wear and tear for the first year the buyer owns the home. Warranties usually offer, at no additional cost, up to one year of coverage while the home is up for sale.

Don't overprice your house. Studies show that 60 percent of all the people who will look at your home come during the first thirty days. If you overprice your house, it will immediately fail to compete with others on the market. Buyers expect certain features for a certain price and eliminate those that do not measure up. Overpriced property remains unsold for a long time, and buyers become wary of even making an offer. They will buy something else while you are waiting to reduce the price. Ultimately, overpricing causes a monetary loss to the seller. Consider what happens after holding on to a house for a year: The market *may* come up to your price in a year, but consider the investment you will have continued to make in your house over that year's period. So *don't overprice your house*.

Make a good first impression. A good first impression, or "drive-up appeal," is very important. So dig out your work clothes and see if you can enlist the help of friends! If necessary, paint the exterior, first scraping any peeling paint. Repair any gutters and trim. Pay particular attention to the entry—replace a worn-out doorbell button or mailbox. Put out a new doormat. Thoroughly weed and prune bushes, and plant some flowers in front. Keep the lawn mowed and trimmed meticulously. Be sure the inside of your home is clean and uncluttered. A do-it-yourself paint job is well worth your investment in time and money, if your house needs it. Be sure the kitchen and bathrooms sparkle.

Be honest about defects. If you have a problem that you don't intend to fix, be candid about it. Tell them that the dishwasher doesn't work. (Most states have seller disclosure requirements anyway.) Yes, some people will be turned off by the prospect of a major repair, but most buyers who otherwise like the home will be philosophical about a problem openly displayed.

Make a list of utility costs. Buyers are usually interested in heating, air-conditioning, and water bills, and it makes a good impression if they don't have to wait several days while you research this information. Have a list of the last twelve months' utility costs ready for them.

Tips for Sprucing and Fixing Up

First impressions and outward appearances, such as your home's exterior, yard, and paint condition are important, but the serious house buyer is going to look further and deeper. Check on the condition of the following:

- *Windows*. If the screens are torn and you don't wish to fix them, remove them entirely. Be sure drapery rods are affixed firmly to the walls and work smoothly. Be sure any shutters, blinds, and drapes work smoothly.
- *Doors*. Repair or replace doors with holes, and be sure all doors open and close freely, including garage doors, sliding glass doors, and closet doors. Don't forget bathroom and kitchen cabinet door hinges.
- *Walls*. Painting will pay dividends out of all proportion to the time and effort spent. Be sure wallpaper is clean and adheres smoothly to walls.

- *Floors*. Tiles or wood should be replaced and polished, and carpet steam-cleaned, with pet odors and stains eliminated. Loose carpet should be restretched and anchored properly.
- *Mechanical and electrical features.* Be sure all light sockets have a good bulb, remembering garage, utility room, halls, closets, and over the stove. The appliances being sold with the house should be in good working order. If specific equipment does not work and you do not intend to repair it, point this out. Dripping faucets and noisy toilets should be fixed, and irreversibly stained or chipped sinks and tubs reenameled. Sprinkler systems should be working properly, with no defective heads.
- *Housekeeping: bathrooms, kitchen, windows, water heater and water softener.* Few things will turn off an enthusiastic buyer faster than dirty bathrooms. Clean vanity, sink faucet, hardware, and mirrors, as well as soap residue in a shower, a moldy shower curtain, the tracks of the shower door, and stained toilet bowls, and replace soiled or missing grout. A buyer will inspect a kitchen carefully, so clean the stove inside and out and replace any stained reflector plates under the heating elements on electric range tops. Don't neglect the exhaust hood. Clean windows are a necessity if the house is to look its best. A sparkling clean water heater or water softener—along with the closet which may house them—is particularly impressive. Be sure heating or air-conditioning filters are clean and ceiling areas around all vents are clean.
- *Arrange for a spacious look.* One of the best ways to improve the show-ability of your home is to open up as much space as possible. "Openness stimulates positive feelings in buyers," declares Roberta Aldridge of Langston Realtors, in Midland, Texas. "You can't change the size of what you have, so try to present it in a pleasing way. If necessary, rent a mini-warehouse to store your excess belongings while your house is on the market. Clean out those closets, so that they will be more than adequate for the clothing stored in them. Throw out the old spices in the kitchen cabinets, and clear out the bathroom cabinets while you're at it. About the garage, it's hard to sell the virtues of a garage when it is filled to

overflowing with twenty-year-old paint cans. Get rid of the debris and add a coat of white paint to the garage! Clean up any oil stains on the garage floor."

Tips for Showings

Sniff out unpleasant odors. Take out all trash and be sure no potatoes or onions are going bad under the sink or in the pantry. Run part of a lemon through the garbage disposal to give it a fresh smell. Move the cat's litter box out of the house. Empty all ashtrays.

Create a light and airy atmosphere. Open all draperies unless there is an objectionable view. Turn on lamps and indirect lighting. (Use overhead lights if that's all there is in that room.) Turn on lights in walk-in closets and leave the door into the walk-in closets slightly ajar to show off this feature.

Replace wet towels and washcloths with clean, dry ones and keep dirty laundry out of the living area.

Get the pets out of the house, if not off the property. Some people don't like animals or are allergic to them.

Get valuables out of sight.

Arrange to be gone, if possible. Most buyers prefer to inspect a home without the owner present. If you're selling the home yourself, give the buyers some time on their own to inspect.

Selling the House Yourself

Be sure to hire a lawyer to advise you and draw up the contract. The contract must give:

- A limitation on the time for a private inspection to be held.
- A limitation on the time the buyers have to secure financing.
- Dates for the closing and title transfer, giving you plenty of time to move.
- A list of items that "go with" the house (curtains, appliances).
- Deposit amount, and the right to keep the deposit if the buyers back out.

Whether working alone or with a real estate agent or broker, be sure you are aware of what the *bottom line results* to you will be—how much money you'll actually receive—as a result of the sale, after all costs are deducted.

A cautionary tale: After several long months of showing her home, Peggy Thorsen finally accepted the offer of a reduced price for her home. When she sat down and subtracted the realtor's fee, an allowance for repairs, homeowners' warranty insurance payment, inspections, and other items, she was shocked. The amount she would actually receive was ten thousand dollars less than she had anticipated!

BUYING A HOME

Can You Really Afford It?

A tried-and-true formula states that the monthly "carrying charge" of your house, which includes the mortgage payment, taxes, and insurance, should not be more than 28 percent of your monthly gross income. The total of your entire debt picture should not exceed 36 percent of your gross income.

You must plan to make a down payment of at least 10 percent of the purchase price of your home, preferably 20 percent. If you make a 20 percent down payment, you probably will not be required to buy mortgage insurance, which costs about 25 percent to 30 percent of the amount of the loan.

See if you can get a lending institution to prequalify you for a loan. Your bargaining power for your dream house will be better if the seller knows you are prequalified, especially when a competing bidder is not.

The Search Is On

As you've heard at least twenty times, the top three considerations in buying a house are location, location, location. If you are relocating to a new area, consider renting for a year while you familiarize yourself with the city and the real estate market.

As you narrow your search, remember:

- Check out the zoning in the neighborhood you're considering. Is it multizoned, so as to allow a factory over on the next street?

- Visit the neighborhood several times. Notice the amount of traffic, noise, and possible smoke or smog.
- Even if you do not have small children, the quality of the schools in the area will be a major factor in the resale of your home.
- Buying the least expensive house in a great neighborhood is considered a better investment than buying the most expensive house in a lesser neighborhood.
- Talk to people you run into in the neighborhood. Get the residents' perspective of what the neighborhood is like.

The Best Time to Buy

Lots of advice is given about the best time to make an offer, including:

- After a property has been on the market several months—or a year.
- August—before school is starting and most buyers have bought and are settled in. Sellers are getting anxious.
- December—when the season is slow and sellers are getting anxious.

Questions to Ask the Realtor or Seller

- What is the quality of the insulation? A good quality rating for insulation for cold climates is R38 for ceilings and R19 for exterior walls. For temperate climates, R22 and R13 respectively.
- Is there termite protection?
- What kind of flooring is under the carpeting? Don't just assume it's something wonderful, like hardwood, just because you saw hardwood in the entry hall.
- What are the utility bills? The less expensive of two homes may turn out to be the more expensive if the utility bills are high.
- What is the age of the appliances that are built in, or go with the sale of the house?
- Are there separate electrical circuits for heating and cooling units and major appliances?

- What is the age of the roof? Is it the original? If not, when was the roof last replaced?

Condominiums, Town Houses, and Cooperatives

A strong trend in the housing market is the movement away from single family homes toward condos, town houses, and co-ops.

When you buy a condo or a town house, you own your home or unit, with a share of the common area of grounds around your home. There is a monthly fee for maintaining, insuring, and paying taxes on the common grounds. When you purchase a cooperative, you are actually buying stock in the corporation that owns the building, and thus gain the right to use your apartment and the common areas. Many cooperatives require that you be approved by the co-op's board of directors before you are allowed to buy stock.

Before buying a town house, condominium, or cooperative, inquire about assessments being considered for repairs. Ask residents if there have been substantial assessments in the past. Look closely at the state of repair of the common areas.

Making an Offer

Your contract should include the following requirements:

- Require that the home be thoroughly inspected by a member of the American Society of Home Inspectors. Plumbing, electrical, and heating and air-conditioning systems, the roof, and the condition of the structure itself should be included in the inspection.
- Include a clause releasing you from buying the house if there are defects in the house.
- Include a clause releasing you from the contract and entitling you to a refund of any deposit if financing is not secured in a certain period of time, say three months.
- Require a title search.
- Require a termite inspection.
- Specify what items are to be left with the house—appliances and window decor, for instance.

Before Making a Loan Application

To expedite the processing of your loan, you will need to look up some information in your files. The following is a list of what you will need:

- Your social security number.
- Your residence address for the last two years.
- Your employer for the last two years.
- Your checking and savings accounts, with the street address of the bank and account numbers.
- The name and address of any accounts that you are presently paying, plus additional closed accounts, for a combined total of at least five credit references covering a two-year period. (Include for each the account number, monthly payment, and balance).
- W-2 forms or tax returns for two years.
- If you currently own real property, you'll need the property address, lender's name and address, account number, value, balance, mortgage cost, rental income, lease, proof of valid title.
- Automobile make, model, year, market value.
- Personal property and household goods value.
- Life insurance type, amount, loan value, monthly payments.
- Name and age of each child (dependent).
- Additional income, rents, credit union, stocks, bonds.
- Child support payments, if applicable.

How to Pay

The number and complexity of mortgages is enough to make your eyes roll back in your head! To determine the best type of mortgage for you, start by estimating how long you think you'll be living in that house, and how long you'll pay on your mortgage. If you will be moving soon, you may be reluctant to tie up a big down payment. Regarding the time and length of the mortgage, the shorter the time over which you pay interest, the better it is for your pocketbook in the long run. However, if you choose a shorter-term mortgage (say a fifteen-year mortgage over a thirty-year), your monthly payments will be significantly higher!

Points. A point is 1 percent of the principal of the loan. Paying points gets you a lower interest rate over the life of a loan. Points, which you pay to the lending institution at closing, are viewed by the IRS as prepaid interest and are consequently tax deductible.

Whether or not points are charged depends upon the policies and requirements of the particular lending institution. Paying points is particularly expensive and unwise if you know you will be in your house for a short period of time. Try to negotiate this issue with the lending institution.

SURVIVAL TIP

When it comes to negotiating the mortgage contract, remember these simple words: *No points is best.*

If you must pay points, then pay the amount of the points separately, by check, directly to the lender. This will give you a receipt for the IRS, showing that this was interest paid to the lending institution (and thereby tax deductible.) Don't lump payment for point charges in with payment of other fees you pay to get the loan.

Conventional mortgages: fixed rate. With a conventional fixed-rate loan, the amount of the monthly payment never changes. Some buyers prefer the comfort of knowing the interest rate will stay the same. These mortgages are particularly desirable when interest rates are low. The downside is that the bank can charge you a higher rate than with adjustable rate mortgages, because of the risk factor that interest rates could go up before the loan is paid off. More interest is charged in earlier years with a conventional loan. You may choose the period of time in which you want to pay off the conventional loan. Remember, the shorter period of time you're paying interest, the better. A case in point:

A local bank has an ad picturing the identical home in two side-by-side photographs. The caption beneath the two photographs reads, "The purchase price of these two houses is the same, but one will cost $80,000 more. The difference? The more expensive home was mortgaged over thirty years, and the less expensive home was mortgaged over fifteen years!" There were lower monthly payments over thirty years, but significantly higher total interest paid.

Adjustable rate mortgages (ARMs). There are over one hundred types of ARMS!

For the first two or three years, the payments of an ARM are lower; by the third year, the rate is as high or higher than a fixed-rate loan. These mortgages, then, are desirable if you know you will be in your home for only a few years, or if interest rates are presently high and you can convert (or refinance) to a fixed-rate mortgage later when interest rates go down. Try to include conversion clauses that allow you to convert to a fixed-rate mortgage without paying points or other conversion costs.

With an adjustable rate mortgage, be sure the mortgage has a set rate above which the interest rates are prohibited from rising—say, not over 2 percent annually and not over 6 percent for the life of the loan.

Prepayment penalty. Check to see if there is a prepayment penalty if the loan is paid off early. You could save significant amounts of money if you should elect at some point to pay off the loan. Remember, using your cash to pay off the mortgage is a good idea only if the interest you're paying on the loan is more than the interest you could earn with the money placed in a safe investment.

Escrow payment. Usually, the loan institution requires one to pay one-twelfth of the year's local taxes and insurance with each monthly mortgage payment. The lending institution earns interest on the escrow funds all year long, paying it out only at the time the insurance premiums and taxes are due. See if your state law and lending institution will allow you to pay the taxes and insurance on your own.

Mortgage insurance. The Federal Housing Administration (FHA) requires mortgage insurance on all its loans. The mortgage insurance premium (MIP) may be financed into the loan. Also, FHA requires a monthly mortgage insurance premium to be paid as a part of the house payment. The up-front payment amount of the premium depends upon the life of the loan. If a loan is for 180 months or less, the up-front amount paid would be .0200 of the loan. For loans of 181–360 months, the up-front amount would be .0225.

The amount of the monthly insurance premium is determined by the life of the loan as well as the amount of the down payment. The more the down payment and the shorter the life of the loan, the smaller the monthly premiums will be.

To give you an example of the longest case scenario with minimal down payment: The longest-term loan for FHA is 30 years. The up-front .0225 MIP for a 30-year loan of $75,000 would be $1,687.50, making the entire loan amount $76,687. The monthly MIP is .005 on a 30-year base loan amount of $75,000, making the monthly premiums $31.25 per month. Two months' monthly MIP must be escrowed at closing.

Conventional loans. For conventional fixed-rate and adjustable rate loans, mortgage insurance is not required when the down payment is at or above 20 percent of the value of the house. Mortgage insurance is required for conventional loans when there is a less-than-20-percent down payment. The buyer with a conventional loan of less than 20 percent of the value of the house has three options:

1. Finance the full amount of the mortgage insurance. (The amount of the loan includes the cost of the mortgage insurance.)
2. Pay an initial premium at closing, two months into escrow, once a month as part of your house payment. (The amount of the loan does not include the mortgage insurance, although the amount is paid as part of your house payment.)
3. Pay the full amount in monthly premiums at a higher rate. (The amount of the loan does not include the mortgage insurance, although the amount is paid as part of your house payment.) This is similar to the renewal premiums in option

2, above; however, the initial premium is eliminated. Two months are collected at closing for deposit to the escrow account.

As with FHA loans, mortgage insurance costs for conventional loans are determined by the life of the loan on your house, as well as the amount of the down payment. The more the down payment and the shorter the life of the loan, the smaller the premiums will be. Mortgage insurance rates vary as to type of payment selected and type of loan—fixed rate or adjustable rate—chosen.

Seminar participants have asked us, "With a conventional loan, when mortgage insurance has been required because a less-than-20-percent down payment has been made on the house, can I cancel my mortgage insurance once I have made enough payments to bring the equity in the house loan up to or over 20 percent?"

Our experts tell us that a borrower may write the lender, provide a current appraisal of the home to reflect that 20 percent equity has been satisfied, and request cancellation of the mortgage insurance; however, it is entirely up to the individual lender as to whether or not you will be allowed to cancel your mortgage insurance. Don't count on it!

Check with your tax expert, your loan expert, and your financial planner to determine your own best course in regard to type of loan and mortgage insurance requirements.

Deciding Whether to Rent, Lease, or Buy

By renting you could invest the money you would have used for a down payment, have the freedom to move without the worry of selling, and avoid the hassle of taking care of the maintenance yourself.

The downside of renting is that you could be sacrificing your privacy, and would be giving up the tax-deductible advantages of interest and property taxes.

When you buy, you accumulate equity in the property. Your

home could become your biggest asset, an asset that could be sold or rented.

When you rent, no part of your monthly payment is set aside for your use and you are not gaining any asset.

In order to gain some benefit (other than daily shelter), you might consider leasing with an option to buy the property. Your monthly payments would be counted against the purchase price so that at least a portion of your rent goes to the purchase. The rent you pay may be used as your down payment, in some instances.

12

New Car Fever

DONNETTE: *Some women, alone for the first time in a long time, find buying a new car thrilling. It's the symbol of a new life, an exciting chance to express who they really are. For others, just looking at the price sticker on the window of a new car is enough to make the knees shake and the heart pound.*

I was lucky. My late husband, Mac, encouraged me to be self-sufficient. He would insist that I personally handle the purchase of my car. I would know how much money I had to work with, of course. Then it was totally up to me to decide which car would best suit my needs at that time in my life, negotiate for the sale or trade-in of my old car, then negotiate for the new car. Sometimes I just wanted to scream at him, "Come help me! You're the lawyer—you can negotiate a heck of a lot better than I can!" But he encouraged me to be self-sufficient.

Mac gave me some tips that I'd like to pass along to you. Here, too, are some that Barbara and I have learned on our own.

Check out the car. When you're beginning to get new car fever, do some research. Read about your car and competing models in magazines such as *Consumer Reports, Car and Driver* and *Motor Trend*. Test-drive the car several times. If this isn't enough, you might try renting the exact model car you're interested in. Be sure that the rental car has similar options to the one you are considering. You might find out it's not what you wanted after all.

Find out the dealer cost. Your first step in negotiating for the car is to find out what the dealer paid the manufacturer for the car. Average markup on a $14,000 to $16,000 car is $250 to $600. For a domestic luxury car, markups range from $600 to $2,500. Be aware that, particularly on luxury cars, the dealer also routinely receives factory rebates or other dealer incentives, so a skillful negotiator-buyer could pay no markup at all. Foreign cars have the highest dealer markup. You can find out dealer cost for a car by calling Intellichoice (1-800-227-2665.) For $14.95 you will receive a computer printout of the dealer cost of the car, including a list of optional features. For only $5.00 more ($19.95) you can get a report on two competing models of cars. You can also check *Consumer Reports* in your local library for information about dealer costs, rebate, and incentives.

Find out the insurance costs. Insurance costs on competing car models may vary as much as 30 percent, due to theft and accident rates. Call your insurance agent to find out what the insurance will be. You can also write to the Insurance Institute for Highway Safety, HLD1 Composite, Box 1420, Arlington, VA 22210, to get information on the claims history of over 170 models of automobiles.

Where and When to Buy

Large high-volume dealers generally have the best deals, if their overhead is not exorbitant. A high-volume dealer in a posh neighborhood may have to charge more to cover his overhead in that location.

August is frequently thought of as being the best time to buy. Bear in mind that the reduced prices reflect only a portion of the first-year depreciation on an "almost-last-year's model." One dealer smilingly admits that he'll happily give a good deal on a convertible in February, when it's been on the lot for four months and no one has even glanced at it for the last two months!

Bargaining

Armed with knowledge of the price the dealer pays the manufacturer for the car, insurance costs, and ideas on where and when to shop, it's time to start making the rounds of the showrooms! Have a list of all the options you want, then duplicate the list so that you have one copy for each dealer you visit. Plan to visit at least three dealers who handle the model you're interested in, and ask for their best cash price for the car. Stress that you want a "drive-it-off-the-lot cash price," including options listed and all fees.

The salesperson will no doubt give you a high price at first, which you will refuse. Then the salesperson will ask what you are willing to pay, at which time you should name the dealer price. He or she will probably refuse, but he or she will know that you are armed with a lot of information, and will counter with a lower price. Ask if this is the rock-bottom price, and explain honestly that you are shopping other dealers for the same model car. If the salesperson will do so, ask him or her to please put the rock-bottom price in writing. You or the salesperson should write the price on the sheet of paper with the options and that dealer's name on it, signed by the salesperson, if he or she consents to the signature. If you decide to trade your old car in, you can return to the dealership later and negotiate this trade.

Car Brokers

Car brokers offer different levels of service. Some brokers offer counseling service, providing you with a consultant who will talk to you on the phone in detail about your wants and needs and make recommendations. The charge is typically $125 to $175 per hour for the consultation only, but only around $100 for up to two hours of guidance time if the consultation is lumped with a complete package which includes buying and service.

The complete package provides you with the latest price lists for the models being considered, with the options available. You make a decision, place an order, and ultimately pick the car up from a factory-authorized dealer near where you live. The fee for the complete package is based on the delivery time—anywhere from twenty-four-hour service to six to twelve weeks for a special factory order. A typical four-week package is $350 to $400 with the broker guaranteeing the absolute lowest price available for the car (or the price of the package is refunded).

Some other broker agencies will provide computerized printouts that give dealer costs and list prices for specified car models, including all options, along with information on rebates, dealer incentives, and special option discounts, usually at a cost of under $20. Then you can use the information desired:

- To negotiate to buy from the dealer of your choice.
- To order the car directly through the broker agency.
- To have the broker agency locate the car at a dealer, then you will negotiate to buy it from the dealer.

If you elect the second or third option, the fee is usually $100 to $125.

Be sure to check with the Better Business Bureau in your area before dealing with a broker. Be sure the broker has been in business for at least five years, has a state license, and has posted a performance bond. Ask the broker for references. Be sure that you pick up your car at an authorized dealership and have your attorney check that the papers show that you are the original and exclusive owner.

SELLING YOUR "OLD" CAR YOURSELF

You can save money by selling your car yourself; however, you must take precautions to protect yourself. First of all, protect your privacy by listing a work number rather than a home number in the ad. Never list your address in the ad. When an interested party calls, gather as much information as you can about the person in advance: full name, daytime and evening phone numbers.

It is best to try to arrange to meet the prospective buyer in a busy public area rather than at home. In any case, be sure to have a friend or relative with you at all times. Get as much identifying information about the buyer as possible, such as a license number. Never get in the car alone with the person; do not allow the person to test-drive or take your car for inspection unless you and a friend or relative are along.

If you make a deal, demand a cashier's check in payment for the car. Do not take personal checks. Meet the buyer at a bank or motor vehicles department to transfer the title before handing over the keys.

AUTOMOBILE LOANS

DONNETTE: *Mac and I kept the first car we bought for nine years. We financed the car, paid it off in three years, then saved money each month until we were able to pay cash for the next car, keeping the nine-year-old car as a second car. You can save hundreds, even thousands of dollars by paying cash for a car.*

If you are financing a car, take the dealership's lowest cash price and shop for the best loan deal you can find. The best deal may be through the car dealership, but check the dealership's finance rate against deals offered by several loan institutions. Pay as much down payment as you possibly can afford and finance the car over as short a period of time as possible. If you are financing through a car dealership and are offered the choice of a rebate or a lower loan interest as part of the deal, it is almost always a better deal for you to take the rebate and put it toward your down payment and pay the higher interest. Double-check the figures for your personal situation, however.

LEASING A CAR

The typical candidate for leasing a car is a person who:

• Wants to drive a new car.
• Has limited funds for up-front cash payment.
• Does not care to own the car.
• Will have minimal wear and tear on the car.

- Drives less than 15,000 miles per year.
- Is the owner of a company who uses the car primarily on company business.

A three-year lease on a $20,000 car would typically require $1,500 initial cash outlay (not including the first month's lease payment) and approximate monthly payments of $283, plus an end-of-lease fee of $100 to $300, plus any wear-and-tear charges. When leasing a car on a three-year, closed-end lease, you have nothing left at the end of the lease. If you had purchased a new $20,000 car, paying a 10 percent or $2,000 down payment, financing the $18,000 loan at 9.5 percent for three years, you would have a three-year-old car worth around $10,500. Of course, your monthly payments would have been significantly higher, approximately $575 per month.

Be leery of leasing companies who run ads for extremely low payments. Read the small print of the deal carefully. There may be requirements for a high down payment, or mileage restrictions, or perhaps the lease is over a longer period of time—say forty-two months.

Leasing Fees

All leases charge acquisition fees unless you've been a long-time valued customer. This fee is usually the first month's payment and one more month as a security fee. Most leases also charge disposition fees of $300 or more.

SURVIVAL TIP

At the end of the lease, you will be charged for "wear and tear" on the car. It's best to have repairs done as you go along, rather than wait until the end of the lease.

Wear-and-Tear Policy

At the beginning of the lease, before you sign on the dotted line, ask the dealer to be as specific as possible about what "wear and tear" means and what you would be charged. Point out a couple of "chinks" in the door of a car on the lot and inquire what you would be charged if you had that type of small dent in the side of the car. What about cigarette burns? Is there a wear-and-tear charge for the smell of cigarette smoke? It will save you money to have repairs done to the car as you go along, rather than waiting until the end of the lease to repair them at the mercy (or lack of mercy) of the leasing company.

Know the dealer's cost. Just as if you were negotiating the price of a new car, find out what the dealer paid the manufacturer for the car you're leasing. A car dealer friend says he is amazed how few people bother to bargain the lease amount, when they would be scrambling for every penny were they buying the car! (Review page 179 of this chapter, "Find Out the Dealer Cost.")

Remember to buy gap insurance. If the car is stolen or totaled, you are liable for the cost of the car. Gap insurance covers the difference between what the car is worth and what is still due on the lease. Although some car-leasing companies include gap insurance in the cost of your lease, many do not. Be sure to inquire.

Keep excess mileage costs down. Before signing the lease, you must assess how many miles you will be driving per month. Miles that are calculated in advance cost around 8 cents per mile, whereas if you drive more than you had predicted, the excess miles cost 10 to 15 cents per mile.

BUYING A USED CAR

The first year's depreciation on a new car is by far the highest of any year thereafter. Some excellent buys can be made on nearly new cars.

"Lemon laws" are designed to protect consumers from getting stuck with a car that may look great but begins to run poorly two days after you've bought it. It's a lot less hassle, however, to do all in your power to protect yourself in the first place. If buying from a used car dealer, ask for the name of the previous owner, call the person, ask what the mileage was when the car was traded, and whether the car had any particular problems. Don't buy the car if you can't get the name of the previous owner. The car might have come from an auto auction, which is where dealers, leasing companies, and rental car agencies send their lemons or badly wrecked cars. (Some good quality cars are handled by auto auctions too.)

Request a thirty-day full warranty to cover all parts and labor. Some dealers offer only 50-50 warranties, in which case you would split the cost with the dealer.

Cars sold by rental car firms are usually last year's models. Prices, warranties, and availability of types of cars vary from company to company. To save time, telephone various rental car companies to see what their policies, prices, and availability are. Because of the bad press rental car agencies have had in the past regarding the quality of their cars for sale, many of them give a service history of the car. Usually, if over $750 has been spent in service, rental car firms will not sell that car directly to the general public, electing to go through an auto auction instead. Ask for a rental period to test the car, say over a weekend. Have your mechanic check the car out, just as you would any other used car you are considering.

SURVIVAL TIP

Before you get in the car, look under where the car is parked. Spots under the engine could signal oil or transmission leaks; spots by the wheels, brake leaks. Drive the car to your mechanic to have it evaluated.

Do your research. As you would with buying a new car, do your homework first. Consumer Reports Used Car Price Service (1-900-446-0500, $1.75 per minute) gives value and past performance data on used car models from 1985 to 1994. The monthly *National Automobile Dealers Association Official Used-Car Guide* lists trade-in (wholesale), loan, and retail values for each make and model and the value of extra equipment.

Negotiate the price on the car. Negotiate the price on the car before having your mechanic check it out. Then insist that any repairs be done free of charge to you. Insist on a test drive.

Check for recalls. Call 1-800-424-9393, the toll-free number of the United States Department of Transportation "Auto Safety Hotline," to find out if your model car has been recalled for any reason. If the car has been recalled and the problem has not yet been taken care of, it can still be repaired at any time, at no cost to you.

Buying a car can be a challenge, but if you do your homework, you'll feel the satisfaction of knowing you managed a successful transaction—and every time you drive your car, you'll feel that satisfaction.

PART III

FROM DOWN THERE
TO UP HERE

13

Traveling

BARBARA: *A recently divorced friend called to share her first experience of traveling alone. She had to drive her car to the Catskills, 120 miles away.*

"I packed as if for a safari," Jane said. "I took a cooler with soft drinks on ice. I got a book on cassette tape. I checked and rechecked the map. Mind you, this was a trip I'd made hundreds of times—but never alone. I thought of every awful thing that might happen, a blowout, carjackers on a lonely road. I got up much earlier than I needed to, changed clothes (right down to the shoes) twice. In the back of my mind there was a nagging little voice that said I shouldn't do this alone, but I had to for the sake of my career.

"I spent the first few miles wishing I had found someone to ride with me. Then, as I started to relax, I popped the cassette into the deck and lost myself in the narration. As the sun brightened the sky, my car tossed the miles aside as if they were nothing. Then I noticed that on each side of the road, the morning sun backlit the wildflowers, and they were absolutely beautiful. All of a sudden I had an elated feeling, almost euphoric, and actually I found the Catskills came too soon. All

*that day, while I did business, I could hardly wait to begin the
long drive home."*

*A small challenge faced that boosted Jane's confidence
beyond measure.*

Women are traveling alone more today than they ever have
before. Besides traveling for pleasure, many have entered the
workforce and their job requires them to travel. If this is a new
experience for you, it can be frightening. With careful planning,
such as making your own reservations for lodging and transportation and by using good judgment, your travel will be a
rewarding experience and something you will look forward to.
Most importantly, it will make you feel self-sufficient.

SURVIVAL TIP

If you travel alone, buy a cellular phone. Just having the
phone beside you will ease your mind, and it can be a real
"lifesaver." Many companies offer reduced rates to customers who use their phones on a limited basis.

TRAVEL ASSISTANCE

Automobile Clubs

To feel more secure in your travel, you might consider joining
an automobile club, such as American Automobile Association
(AAA) (1-800-765-0766). They provide trip routings, travel
guidebooks, insurance, bonding, and emergency repair service
for their members. AAA's nationwide emergency service enables
members to get help almost anywhere in the United States at any
time. Even if you wake up some morning at home and find you
have a dead battery, they will come and assist you.

Travel Agents

Travel of any kind, whether it is for business or a vacation,
does not have to be as expensive as you think. Again, the key is in

the planning. Travel agents are paid by the hotel or the airline. Not by you. Many times it is easier to use a travel agent because they have all the latest information on special discounts and rates for lodging, transportation, tours, schedules, etc., at their fingertips in the computer. However, if you have the time, make the arrangements yourself. Sometimes, through persistence, the hotel or the airline will find reservations for an individual that they will not for a travel agent. Most companies have toll-free phone numbers you can get by calling 800 information (1-800-555-1212). It can be such fun to see just what a good deal you can get. Also, most state bureaus of tourism and travel have toll-free numbers, as do the convention and visitors' bureaus of large cities.

TAKING A PLANE

Air fares

Pay for your ticket when you make your reservations. Prices are always subject to increase, and the quoted price may go up by the time you actually travel.

SURVIVAL TIP

Consider obtaining a special credit card which will earn free airline travel for every dollar you charge to the card.

If you use one of these credit cards, plan to pay your bill in full each month, because these cards usually carry a higher interest rate.

- Discounted fares are often subject to penalties if you ask to change flights. Many times they are also nonrefundable. Make sure you understand before you pay.
- You could save hundreds of dollars simply by staying over a Saturday night. Try to be flexible.
- Airlines offer discounts to senior citizens. Don't be too proud to pass up this opportunity to ask for significant savings.

SURVIVAL TIP

After purchasing your ticket and before you fly, check to see
if the fare has decreased. Sometimes, for a small fee, like
$25, you can get the lower fare.

Baggage

The best way to make sure an airline does not lose your
baggage is to carry it on the airplane with you. However, when
that is impossible, do the following:

- Place tags with your name and address on the inside as well as
  the outside of each bag. If possible, use a business address, not
  a personal address.
- Lock your bags. This will not prevent your bag from being
  stolen, but it will prevent it from coming open.
- Carry on the plane such items as medicine, jewelry, your
  contact lenses and glasses, and any other items that you
  cannot afford to lose.
- Watch the attendant to make sure that they have put the
  correct baggage check tags (for destination and flight number) on your luggage.
- If your luggage fails to appear, notify the airline personnel
  immediately. Be sure to fill out the claim form that they give
  you correctly. If your bags and contents are worth more than
  $750, the amount the airline is liable per bag, consider buying
  extra-valuation insurance at the check-in counter or check
  your homeowner policy for baggage insurance.
- Make an inventory describing each bag and its contents and
  keep it with you, separate from the baggage.

TAKING A TRAIN

Rail travel remains an economical way to see the country.
Amtrak covers over 24,000 miles in forty two states and Canada.
There are discount fares for senior citizens, the handicapped,

and military personnel, and some select family discounts. For information on Amtrak routes and fares, call 1-800-USA-RAIL.

RENTING A CAR

Car rental rates vary according to such things as time (midweek, weekend, number of days), mileage, and whether you will return the car to the original location. Another consideration is whether the car should be returned with a full tank of gasoline or empty. We have a friend, Shelley, who recently rented a car, and the attendant suggested she return the car empty. When she did, her bill was $99 rather than the $54 it would have been if she'd filled the tank herself at a regular gas station. Shelley complained to the president of the company and received an apology and a refund. *Never* be reluctant to question your bill if there are charges that you do not agree with.

When you are quoted a price, always ask for a better deal. Usually, better deals are available. Compare the prices of all the major firms (listed in the yellow pages with 800 numbers). Many smaller rental companies are building impressive rental networks in major cities, and they often have surprisingly low prices. You may receive a discount by presenting the ticket from the airline, if there is a prearrangement with the rental agency. Check airline in-flight magazines for special coupons and price offers.

When renting a car remember:

- Always rent in advance of your trip to make sure you will get a car. Many times cars will not be available because of some event that you are not aware of.
- Many times, weekend rates mean from Thursday noon through Sunday or possibly until Monday noon. If you will need the car for only a few hours into the next twenty four hours, ask if the cost can be prorated.
- Find out if your own auto insurance will cover rental cars; if so, do not pay extra charges. Be sure to check to see if your policy covers rental car theft.
- Always take proof of your liability insurance in case you have an accident while driving a rented car.

HOTELS

Many hotels today look more like resorts—with pools, exercise rooms, gift shops, and nightclubs. If you need only a place to spend the night, look for a hotel without these amenities and a lower room rate.

Make your reservations as far in advance as possible to get special rates. When you register, confirm the discount. These discounts could be for senior citizens, families, or for corporate, military, or car club membership. Weekend discounts are often available at hotels and resorts that cater to business travelers during the week. Three-day packages may offer a 30 percent savings and include extras such as theater tickets, drinks, and tours. When you check out, remind the clerk of the discount before the bill is totaled.

Overbooking is now a common hotel practice. When making your reservations, always insist upon a confirmation number. Better still, guarantee payment for a reserved room in advance by giving the hotel your credit card number for billing. Should your plans change, you can cancel this reservation by notifying the hotel. Usually, such cancellations must be made by an appointed time, say twenty-four hours in advance. Ask the hotel clerk for details when confirming.

If it is necessary to extend your stay longer than planned, remember that a hotel usually will not evict a guest if that guest has paid his bill or established credit.

MONEY-SAVING VACATIONS

Rebate Travel Agencies

This service is for the traveler who likes to plan her own trips.

First, contact the tour, cruise, or flight and plan the trip with preferred scheduling. Then call the rebate travel agency with the details. They make all your bookings and then calculate the total cost of your trip. They then deduct the commission (usually 10 percent), add their appropriate booking fee, and advise you of the total net cost. Because of their high volume, they are able to offer special rates with carriers.

The rebate travel agency provides the tickets and vouchers, and passes the savings on to you. And of course, the more expensive the trip, the greater the savings the agency can provide for you. Two of these firms to consider are The Smart Traveler (1-800-448-3338) and Travel Avenue (1-800-333-3335).

Discount Travel Services

If you are able to travel on short notice, there are firms that cater to you. They offer unsold space and tickets on cruise lines, charter flights, and tours at savings up to 67 percent, or even more, as departure time nears.

These are guaranteed reservations. They charge an annual membership fee, usually $30 to $45. Two of these firms to consider are Vacations to Go (1-800-338-4962) and Stand-Buys (1-800-255-0200).

Travel Clubs

Travel clubs are wonderful for anyone whose schedule can be rearranged to take advantage of special trips throughout the year. However, before paying a membership fee, ask for information on the following items:

- Participating hotels and airlines.
- Size of the discounts. You might be able to get a better discount on your own, especially if you are a senior citizen.
- Method of payment.
- Total cost. Many times all the optional, related, and service charges can pad the price of a discount vacation.

Club fees usually range from $30 to $60 and include brochures or hotlines explaining upcoming trips. Some better-known firms that have been in business for many years are Encore (1-800-887-2963) and Sears Discount Travel Club (1-800-331-0257).

FOREIGN TRAVEL

If you're going to leave the country, you may need a passport. If you do not have a passport, be sure to apply for it *well* in advance of your trip. Processing your application can take more than six weeks.

Passport Tips

- You don't have to look like a ghoul in your passport photo. When you have the photo taken, pick a picture you like. It will haunt you for the next ten years.
- If you already have a passport, be sure you renew it before it expires. It is much easier to renew than to start all over again.
- Keep your passport with you on your trip. Don't leave it in your room while you're out sightseeing. Leave a photocopy of the passport picture page and passport number back in the room. If the actual passport is lost, replacement will be faster if you have a copy of the picture page and passport number.
- If your passport is stolen or lost, report it immediately. If lost in the United States, notify local police authorities and Passport Services Office, Washington, D.C. 20520-4818, or, if overseas, the nearest American embassy or consulate.
- Be sure that you've given your passport number to a friend back home. An easy way to keep all the information easily accessible is to photocopy the passport and leave the copy with a friend.

Money

Traveler's checks are a practical way to carry money. Get them in small denominations and keep a copy of their numbers in a separate place.

Remember that you've got to get your traveler's checks converted to money as soon as you arrive. Be aware of banking hours in each town you visit. Usually, hotels and airports have banks that will make the conversion for you, but at much less favorable rates than at regular banks.

You can make charges on your credit cards without making the conversion from foreign to American dollars. However, it's a good idea to check the total yourself and calculate the amount to make sure you're not being overcharged.

Foreign Electricity

Voltage in foreign countries is often 220V, different from the 110V which is standard in the United States. Usually, even the wall plugs are of different configuration from our own. Adaptor kits, which convert electricity so that you may use your electric conveniences, such as hair dryer and curling iron, are available in luggage shops or luggage departments of department stores.

Occasionally, the adaptors do not work as well as one would wish. To save wear and tear on your nerves (as when, for example, the electric current of your hair dryer sometimes works and sometimes doesn't), you might want to invest in a hair dryer or curling iron after you arrive at your foreign destination.

Phoning Home

The most expensive way to call home is from your hotel. Most hotels add their own charge to your bill. Two of our friends were shocked when the bill for a call home was presented at their German hotel. The total was $87 for a short call—and they had to pay cash for it, on the spot.

Consider using one of the newer around-the-world calling services. You'll be charged for membership in it, but if you or members of your family are going to be overseas, it may be worth it.

America is just now getting on the bandwagon of phone calling cards. These are prepaid debit cards with a designated amount of worth which can be used for phone calls. A $15 or $30 calling card may be all you need while you're traveling. Different configurations of cards are used abroad, so wait until you reach your foreign destination to purchase a phone debit card to be used in that country.

SURVIVAL TIP

Phone calling cards make great presents for your traveling friends.

PREPARING FOR ANY TRIP

Before you go on a trip, leave this information with a friend or relative:

- Your itinerary, with phone numbers if possible.
- Your traveler's check numbers.
- Credit card account numbers and telephone numbers.
- Checking account numbers and bank telephone number.
- Photocopies of your passport, driver's license, and health insurance cards.

There are other items that would be worth organizing and recording before you go on a trip:

- Eyeglass prescriptions.
- Generic name of prescription medications.
- Official copy of birth certificate.
- Copies of "green cards," special entry visas, travel insurance forms.
- Names and phone numbers of relatives who would like to be informed about your travels.

The more you organize in advance, the easier your trip will be. However, don't allow the small details to keep you from going. Once you realize you can go anywhere and do anything you want, even *alone*, you'll be on the road and there will be no stopping you!

14

Socializing and Dating Again

SOCIALIZING AGAIN

DONNETTE: *We are always happy to hear women in our work-shops display an interest in "reentering the human race," as one woman smilingly expressed it. In fact, one of our most fre-quently asked questions goes something like this: "I really miss being included with my old group of married friends. I am included for lunch with the women, but I am excluded from dinner and theater parties with the husbands. What can I do about this?"*

So here are some tips for socializing again:

- **Plan some dinner parties of your own.** You might ask a male friend to cohost, or just be your helper to mix the drinks or keep an eye on the burgers on the grill. Invite your "old group" to be your guests.
- **Let friends know you are available to go out,** and can be ready without a lot of advance notice. Then if someone is unable to use tickets that were purchased for an event, you'll be in line for them.
- **You don't need a man in order to go out.** If you love the theater or the ballet, *go* to the theater or ballet. Many of your

friends sit at home because their husbands don't like the same entertainment they do. Invite one of these women to go with you to something you'll both enjoy.

• **Don't be self-conscious about going places alone.** *Research by the Milwaukee-based Davis and Associates reveals that by the year 2007 more than half of all American adults will be single.*

• **Look for opportunities to make new friends.** Join a study group at your church. Volunteer with museum, symphony, art, or ballet associations, if this is your interest. Take up tennis again, if you enjoyed it at one time. Keep a list of the people you meet with whom you feel kinship. Next time you feel like running out for dinner and a movie, call one of your new friends.

SURVIVAL TIP

Become comfortable going places alone! Recent research has shown that food, travel, and hospitality industries are beginning to cater to the single adult. You are in demand!

DATING AGAIN

It is not infrequent that after a "Life Strategies" seminar, a woman will timidly approach us and say, "I haven't dated for years. I feel like a bumbling teenager. How do you go about dating in this day and age?"

Before considering the logistics of the first date itself, we suggest that you do a little self analysis. There are some wrong reasons for wanting to date again, and right reasons for wanting to date again. It's wise to consider how to go about meeting men, and to think about how to overcome some of the obstacles that may arise when you begin dating again.

Wrong Reasons for Starting to Date Again

• You cannot support yourself financially and you need a man to pay the way.
• You are afraid of—or very uncomfortable with—being alone.

- You want someone else to make decisions for you.
- Your friends are nagging you.
- You want to show your ex you are still attractive to men.
- Having a man around makes you feel more secure, and anyone's better than no one.

Right Reasons for Starting to Date Again

- You are ready for a man's company, as opposed to his financial aid, because you have established that you can make it on your own financially.
- You have overcome most of your bitterness and/or grief. Look back over the sections on grief in chapter 2, "Divorced," and chapter 3, "Widowed." Some of us need some professional help dealing with bitterness and grief, and if you need help, by all means, seek good professional counseling.
- You have no desire to settle for *just any* man. You desire the companionship of a man whom you respect, whose interests are of interest to you.
- You will choose whom you continue to date. By no means would you think, "Anything's better than nothing!"

Overcoming Some Obstacles to Dating

You might feel ready to start dating, and the conditions might be perfect, but there are some concerns that stand in your way. Let's consider some of these obstacles and how they can be remedied.

You feel nervous. Rest assured, it's normal to feel nervous at the prospect of dating again! To control some of those butterflies in your stomach, why not look upon your first date as an opportunity to make a new friend, or to learn more about a new acquaintance. Often, the most satisfactory romantic relationships are those in which there is first true friendship. So forget the concept of romantic involvement for now. Develop a new friend. If he isn't worth being your friend, he's certainly not worth being a future romantic partner!

Your children object. Your children may object to the mere concept of your dating. Their objection could stem from several emotions. First, your children may feel honest concern for your well-being, or fear that you may make an undesirable choice of a stepfather for them. Didn't (or wouldn't) you feel the same concern for their futures when they were (or will be) dating? Assure them that you, too, want no choices that are unwise for your—and their—futures. Tell them (and mean it) that you wouldn't date any type of person you wouldn't want them to date! Your children may feel jealousy. Assure them of their importance in your life and then explain the need for a new dimension in your life. Be kind but firm about this.

You feel self-conscious about the way you look. If it's something you can do something about, then start now. Get a new haircut. Start wearing more stylish clothes. Exercise—walk the mall! Join a healthy weight-loss group. Treat yourself to a cosmetic makeover, often offered free of charge at cosmetic counters eager to have you as a new client.

Meeting Men

DONNETTE: *At a recent seminar, several of the women present were whispering among themselves during the question-and-answer period. After a short period of giggling, one of the whispering group raised her hand and said, "Donnette, we notice you're wearing a shiny new wedding band. How'd you meet him?"*

"My experience was just pure dumb luck," I admitted. "I was walking the mall one evening after work, rounded a corner, and practically collided with Ron. I had not seen Ron in quite some time. It had been ten years since we had first met each other through playing in tennis tournaments. We chatted briefly, and I learned that he, too, had been single for some time. Later that evening, he called me for a date."

Although pure dumb luck is always a possibility, networking and participating in activities you enjoy with others is likely to increase your chances of meeting someone with whom you share mutual interests. Some suggestions:

- If you enjoy sports, join a tennis or golf group, or sign up for lessons. If cultural events are more to your liking, join the local symphony, drama, art, or jazz music associations. Museums are constantly recruiting new members, and upon joining a museum you will be on the list for openings of all new exhibits. Go! If you like to write, join a writer's club. Every newspaper has weekly listings of activities. Stay current with what's going on in your community.

- Have you intended to start back to church, but just haven't made it yet? Go ahead, go back to church. Visit Sunday school classes and church study groups until you find one with which you feel comfortable. Often extracurricular church activities—such as Sunday school classes and study groups— are small and offer you the opportunity of getting to know others on a more personal level.

- If your best friend suggests a friend—described as a really neat guy—for a blind date, take a chance. Accept the invitation. You might share some things in common or you might not. You might get some new ideas—a new slant on a topic of interest. Maybe you'll even hear of a job opportunity! You never have to go out with him again if things don't click.

- Parent Teacher Association (PTA) and children's activities offer excellent opportunities for meeting new friends, male or female.

- If you can afford to travel, do so. Research travel tours, cruises, and travel clubs which include people of your age and interest range.

- For years you've received notices of class reunions, but you've never gone. This year make up your mind to go!

SURVIVAL TIP

Common sense for your safety: If you are meeting an Internet pen pal or a blind date from the personals in the classified ads for the very first time, be sure that you are in a public place or with good friends as your chaperones.

THE DATE

Times have changed. It's considered okay for women to call men on the phone and invite them for a date. But we're still "of the old school" and personally would feel uncomfortable with making the first call to ask a man for the first date. So if you're uncomfortable with doing the "first asking," we understand!

One suggestion for feeling more comfortable—if it's the first date and you're doing the asking—is to ask the man to meet you for a *daytime* activity—such as a casual lunch. Also, you may feel more at ease inviting him for the first time by saying, "I have two tickets for the theater Wednesday evening" (where you will be in the company of numerous other people), rather than asking him to a small, dimly lit restaurant for dinner! If you ask once and are turned down, leave it alone for a while—he knows you're interested, so leave the ball in his court. Never show that you're desperate, because you're not!

Who Pays?

A good rule of thumb is that whoever does the asking does the paying. If you're doing the asking, and you wish the date to be Dutch treat, then make it known when you're inviting him. If he's doing the asking, and you are unsure as to whether or not he's paying, then ask. Whoever pays, expect and make it clear that no obligations are due to anyone just because he or she picks up the tab!

Eight General Rules

1. While you're getting dressed to go out on the date, turn on the news. Make a mental note of three current events to discuss in case there are awkward periods of silence.
2. Do not talk about your ex on a first or second date.
3. Show yourself to be the positive-thinking person you are. None of us likes to hear others' stories of grief, bitterness, and anger—especially on early dates. Spare him a litany of your aches and pains. Save long stories about your past for further-in-the-future dates, when it is more appropriate to share more about yourself, if you both wish to do so.

4. If you have children, don't talk about them and show pictures of them all evening. Certainly, it's fine to mention your children and show how much you love them, but don't make the children your only contribution to the conversation.

5. Be a listener as well as a contributor to the conversation. Show that you are interested in what he is saying. Be responsive and do your share of the talking, but do not dominate the conversation. If he dominates the entire conversation and shows no interest in what you have to say, you likely will have no interest in being with him again.

6. Don't make snap decisions based on the first date. If he did talk a little too much, perhaps he was just nervous. If he has some interests that are different from yours, this could be a good thing. If you find after a few dates that your interests are entirely different, then you would certainly not want to continue dating him.

DONNETTE: *My husband Ron's "techy-ness" and proficiency with computers encouraged me to become more proficient with computers myself, and has helped immensely with my writing and seminar presentations. Ron is forever telling me how thankful he is for my years of experience as an interior designer, an interest he'd never developed for himself!*

7. If he perceives you to be a workaholic or a social butterfly because you are always too busy to be with him, it's likely he'll look elsewhere. So, if you've determined you'd like to see more of him, don't play *too* hard-to-get.

8. Above all, remember, "We teach people how to treat us." You are about to be in the process of dating for the pleasure of male companionship. You are *not* in the business of making yourself into whatever someone else wants you to be. Be your own person. This does not mean you should not reveal your admirable characteristics of kindness, consideration for others, and willingness to do your share of being flexible and giving. It does mean, however, that you should maintain your self-respect, and consequently deserve the respect of others.

SURVIVAL TIP

Judging by the experiences of our workshop participants, more and more invitations are extended for a weekend out of town. We would insist on separate rooms, with a clear understanding of who will pay. Be sure to leave the address and phone number of where you will be with friends and relatives.

GETTING SERIOUS

Getting to know each other in a variety of circumstances prior to marriage gives us higher odds for making a successful marriage. You should date him long enough to be sure of your commitment to him and of his commitment to you. Many family and marriage counselors advise dating for a year to two years prior to marriage. (As for cohabitation before marriage, we believe that if you're going to live with a man, you should be married to him.)

Here are some considerations to help you decide if the two of you will be compatible:

- What are his spiritual beliefs? Does he have any? Are they compatible with yours? Does he have respect for your spiritual beliefs?
- How patient and flexible is he when things don't go his way?
- What is he like when he's sick?
- What are his interests? Is he a TV addict or a golfaholic? How much time does he relegate to his extracurricular activities? Does his job consume all his time? It's not necessary for all your interests to be alike, but his addiction to the tennis court or the Internet can be almost as frustrating as a substance addiction!
- Avoid like the plague anyone who is abusive—either to you or who abuses drugs or alcohol!
- What is his commitment to his family? If he has children, how interested is he in his children? If you have children, how do

your two families meld? Have you met his parents, brothers, and sisters? What are his attitudes and obligations toward his parents? How does he treat his mother and sister? How would you describe his attitude toward women in general?

- What are his vacation interests? Where does he prefer to spend the holidays? Is he totally set in his ways about his own past holiday and vacation traditions, unwilling to incorporate any of your own traditions?

- Do you dislike his housekeeping habits or the way he dresses but think you'll change all that when you marry him? Don't count on it!

- What is his attitude toward money? Is he a spendthrift to the point that you wonder if he's trying to impress you with his flamboyance? Is he miserly? Does he show an interest in planning for the future, such as putting the kids through college and retirement? Has he tried to get you to loan him money? (The right answer to that: *no*.) Will he discuss money with you? See the next portion of this chapter, "Prenuptial Agreements," for tips on how to share financial information with each other.

- Trust your intuition. If for any reason you have doubts about the man of your dreams, discuss it with your pastor or counselor. If there is mystery about him that makes you uncomfortable, look elsewhere!

PRENUPTIAL AGREEMENTS

Attorneys and financial advisers frequently recommend a legal prenuptial agreement for couples who have a significantly large number of separate assets or have children by a previous marriage whose financial future they wish to protect. A prenuptial agreement will specifically spell out how joint assets would be divided and separate property would be treated if the couple were to divorce. A prenuptial agreement can be so specific as to delineate how the husband's and wife's incomes are divided during their marriage.

Regardless of your decision regarding a formal prenuptial agreement, be very sure that you are aware of your future husband's financial situation prior to your marriage, and be willing to be open with him about your own finances. If he was previously married, he may have substantial financial obligations to his prior wife and family. Are there alimony payments? Child support payments? What are his financial obligations to his children, regardless of their age? Will he be paying for college educations? What are his assets, and what are his debts?

Before Donnette married, Ron voluntarily produced his personal financial statement, and she was happy to show hers to him. Shortly before they were married, they revised their wills and had durable powers of attorney and powers of attorney for health care revised, naming each other as the one who would have the power of attorney in the event of the incapacitation of the other.

Be sure that you become comfortable discussing finances with each other. Barbara laughingly tells our workshop participants that when her two daughters were teenagers, they led their parents to believe that they were totally incapable of balancing their checkbooks. After the young women married several years later, they both announced to Barbara that they were handling the finances of their households. "Frankly," says Barbara, "this bit of news struck terror to my heart the first time they told me, *but* believe it or not, everything runs very smoothly. Before they married, they established real partnerships with their husbands by discussing how all money would be spent...and to this day they each have a real friendship and a real partnership with their husbands."

Take a worthwhile tip from Barbara's daughters. Discuss with your fiancé what the household budget will be and specifically who will be paying for each line item in the budget. Discuss saving and investing for the future and for your retirement together. Where are his insurance policies filed? (Automobile, health, homeowners, life.) Where is his health insurance card? Does he have life insurance? Who is the beneficiary? Who will be the beneficiary after your marriage? What are his investments? Does he have a pension plan? One of the major topics of arguments—and one of the major reasons cited for divorce—is money. You don't want to be one of the negative statistics. Do yourself a favor. Establish a friendly partnership regarding the business and finance of marriage!

One of the most frequently asked questions during our workshops is, "How do I get my fiancé to answer my questions about our future finances?"

If this is a problem for you, we suggest that you make an appointment with your fiancé to discuss what you would like to learn about each other's finances. Make the appointment for lunch, or for a meeting in his office. Don't pop financial questions over a romantic dinner in a dimly lit restaurant, or when he's in a hurry to get to a ball game. Before you go to your meeting with him, be sure that you're well prepared. Look at all of the questions in the above paragraphs. Which of these questions do you need answers to? Make a list of questions you have about his financial business, and be sure you are well aware of your own financial situation to share with him. Type the list so that it looks very businesslike. Dress in a businesslike manner to portray your businesslike intentions. Drag out your navy blue suit!

When you broach the subject, use "I need" and "I feel" terminology. "Tom, I need to feel secure about all facets of our future together, and I want you to feel secure too. There are some financial questions that, for my peace of mind, I need answers to, and I need your help." Avoid accusatory terminology, such as, "Every time I bring up money, you clam up, and I'm sick of it." Reassure him that you want him to know about the financial side of your life too.

Our experience has been that he will not feel threatened by systematically going through a list of objective questions, especially when you have offered to share similar personal financial information as well. We have received word back from several of our workshop participants about our find-out-before-you-have-to-know advice. This letter from Carrie is perhaps the most poignant:

Dear Donnette and Barbara,

Seven months ago, I attended one of your seminars at the college. I was the person who asked the question about how to get my fiancé to divulge financial information and discuss future budgeting. In the two years I'd dated him, I had come to know that he is a loving, giving, and generous person. But I had been unsuccessful in getting him to talk about money and our future financial security, and it was causing no small amount of resentment in me.

I followed your advice to the letter. I called Brent at his office to make an appointment to see him in his office to discuss a number of questions you'd brought up in the seminar. I typed a list of questions—the ones that were relevant to us and our situation. At the meeting, he was not at all reluctant to discuss a specific list of questions that he could see on paper. He agreed that it was an excellent idea to draw up new wills and execute durable powers of attorney for health care, which we did a couple of days before we married and left on our honeymoon.

I'm writing to say thank you, thank you. While we were on our honeymoon, someone ran a red light and crashed into the driver's side of the car. Brent was in a coma for five days. Thanks to our "finances" discussion, I knew where his health insurance card was in his wallet! I knew where the automobile insurance policy was filed. Thanks to God, Brent came out of the coma, and I never had to make the decisions allowed me by the durable power of attorney for health care. The first weeks were slow and painful; however, at least I knew where the savings account was, and could handle our fiscal responsibilities alone for a while. Thank you again. Brent and I are most appreciative for the excellent advice.

Warmest Regards,

Carrie Paschall

15

Onward and Upward

BARBARA: *As Donnette and I prepared this last chapter we reminded each other of the time back at the beginning of our transition. Mac had just died and I was getting my divorce. We were petrified by the realization of our lack of knowledge. Donnette would read something about financial planning and share it with me. I would talk with someone about health insurance and share that information with Donnette. We helped each other gain the knowledge we needed to feel secure. We used to laugh and say we looked forward to the day we could read for pleasure rather than always reading something we felt we needed to know!*

After developing our Life Strategies seminars, we received some excellent questions and suggestions from our seminar participants on material that had not been covered in our seminars. We are including some of their suggestions, questions and answers in the quiz section of this chapter.

QUIZ AND SHORT REVIEW

Car Purchase and Maintenance (see chapter 12, "New Car Fever")

Can you negotiate for the purchase of a new car?

Consumer Reports, found at your public library, gives detailed assessments of domestic and foreign automobiles.

What about buying a used car?

Call Consumer Reports Used Car Price Service at (900) 446–0500 ($1.75 per minute), which gives value and past performance data (repair history, etc.) on used cars.

How often should your tires be rotated?

Some manufacturers suggest, to extend the life of your tires, you should have them rotated every 7,500–8,000 miles.

How often should the oil be changed in your car?

Some automobile manufacturers recommend every 3,000 miles.

Health (see chapter 5, "Teaching Others How to Treat You")

How can one "check up" on a doctor?

Call Medi-Net at (888) 275-6334 or find them on-line at http// www.askmedi.com; the fee is $15 for one name, $5 for each additional name requested during a call or on-line hit. You will be able to find out whether he or she has been disciplined for billing fraud, overprescribing, incompetence, or some other transgression. The records are updated daily.

How often should a woman see her gynecologist?

Every year for a pap smear and breast exam. Most gynecologists suggest that women over the age of forty have yearly mammograms.

How important is exercise?

Very, not only for your physical being but for your mental attitude. You will be surprised how exercise lifts your spirit. *Make it a priority.*

Home Suggestions

Locate the main cutoff valves for the water and gas in your home.

Label the switches in your electrical breaker box.

Change your heating/air conditioning filters regularly.

Before leaving home for extended periods, unplug nonessential appliances like TVs, computers, toasters, and room air conditioners, which can cause fires.

Do not leave the house when the clothes dryer is on.

Malfunctioning dryers are the leading cause of appliance-related house fires.

Insurance (see chapter 10, "Protecting Your Assets")

Review your policies annually to be sure your policies meet your needs.

Do you need life insurance?

If you have no one depending on you for their livelihood, you may not need life insurance.

Have you chosen a low deductible on your auto insurance in order to save money on your premiums?

If you raise the deductible from $200 to $500, you will save 20 percent of the premium you would pay if your deductible were $200. Increase it from $200 to $1,000 and save 45 percent.

Do you need a new health insurance policy?

Be sure to have a new policy in place before canceling your old one. If you have been covered under your husband's health insurance and you divorce or he dies, there are laws issued by the Department of Labor (COBRA) that require his firm to offer insurance coverage to you and your family for thirty-six months. However, you will pay the group rate yourself.

Money (chapter 10, "Protecting Your Assets")

Can you balance your checkbook?

Consult your local bank for a crash course.

Do you pay your bills on time?

Paying bills on the first and fifteenth of every month will keep your credit in good order.

Do you know your credit rating?

To order a free copy of your report, call 1-800-682-7654.

Have you established a line of credit with a bank?

(See chapter 2, "Divorced," and chapter 10, "Protecting Your Assets.")

Do you have a credit card in your legal name? What is your legal name?

It is important that you get a credit card in your own name and use your legal name on the credit card. If your maiden name was Jane Doe and you married John Smith, your social title may be Mrs. John Smith, but it isn't considered your legal name. Your legal name might be your first name plus your maiden (birth) name, Jane Doe, or your first name, maiden name and married last name, Jane Doe Smith. You can even revert to your maiden name easily if you wish. As long as you keep the same social security number, the legal system does not have a problem with the last name you choose to use. You do go to court to have it done, though. If you are divorcing, it can be done at the time of your divorce.

Do you maintain a current list of your credit cards and their numbers?

An easy way to keep a list is to lay them on a copy machine and copy them. If you lose your pocketbook, you will be glad you took the time to do this. Remember to copy both front and back. The back of the card lists the telephone number to call if the card is lost.

What are your outstanding debts and percentage of interest on each?

If the interest on your debts is more than the interest you are earning on a savings account, pay off your debt with the savings! Then start saving again.

Do you have a mortgage on your home?

Pay as little as $25 extra a month on a thirty-year, fixed-rate, 8 percent mortgage and you will save $23,337 over the life of the loan. Pay an extra $100, and you will save $62,456.

What can you do if you find yourself in debt?

To get free or low-cost help for credit problems, call Consumer Credit Counseling Services at 1-800-388-2227 for a referral to an office near you.

Are you planning for retirement? Saving/investing monthly toward that goal?

Women's life expectancy in the United States is seven years longer than men's, so they must accumulate more savings simply to carry them through their lifetime.

How much should you be saving of your total gross income?

Some financial planners advise for maximum financial security; you should begin early in life to save 7 to 10 percent of your total gross income.

How much cash should you keep accessible for emergencies?

Some financial planners suggest at least three months' worth of your regular expenses.

Do you keep a list of assets?

See chapter 10, "Protecting Your Assets."

Spouse Benefits

Who shares in the pension plan?

Since 1974 there has been a series of laws that have mandated a spouse's right to share in a pension fund. If your spouse has a private pension plan that is paid out in the form of a fixed monthly benefit, you are entitled to *no less than one half,* should you divorce. (See chapter 2, "Divorced.") As a widow, you may have to decide how you will receive pension benefits from your husband's employer. Usually, you can choose to receive the full amount in a lump sum or lifetime payments. This is not the time to make a hasty decision. Consult a financial planner to see what the best plan would be for your situation.

Can a pension plan be divided, when a couple divorces, without penalty?

In the event of divorce, the Internal Revenue Code allows a procedure called a "qualified domestic relations order" (QDRO) to distribute, segregate, or otherwise recognize the attachment of any portion of a participant's benefits in favor of the participant's spouse, former spouse, or dependents without violating the restrictions on alienation of benefits. (Only a spouse, former spouse, child, or other dependent of a participant may be an "alternate payee" under a qualified domestic relations order.) This procedure is highly technical and you must rely on the advice of your tax counsel and attorney.

Is a woman entitled to some of her husband's social security if divorced or widowed?

If a couple was married longer than ten years, a former wife, who is unmarried, is entitled to her former husband's benefits. If a widow is at least sixty years old but under sixty-five, she may claim social security benefits. However, the amount she will receive will be significantly lower than that which she would receive if the payments start after the age of sixty-five. For information contact the Social Security Administration at 1-800-772-1213 on weekdays from 7:00 A.M. to 7:00 P.M. They will be able to answer most of your questions.

Taxes

Can you question your property-tax bill if it seems excessive?

According to the National Taxpayers Union, about 60 percent of homes in America are overassessed. Call the American Homeowners Association at (888) 470-2242 and order *The Homeowners Property Tax Reduction Kit.*

Does one need a tax preparer whose office is open year around?

If you are audited, you need someone to go with you to answer questions. Part-time tax preparers may not be available. Also, you may need tax questions answered throughout the year.

Wills (see chapter 10, "Protecting Your Assets")

Do you have an up-to-date will?

If you do not do another thing as a result of this book, make an up-to-date will. If you do not have one, the state where you live has one for you in the event of your death!

Have you made provision for guardians for your children?

If you have not done so, the state in which you reside will choose guardians for you.

Have you asked the executor of your will if he or she is willing to serve in this capacity?

Being an executor is a big job. Be sure your executor understands the scope of the job.

Does the executor of your will know where your will is located?

Some states permit you to leave the original of your will in your safe-deposit box. Laws in other states require the executor to have the original of your will in order to get into the safe-deposit box.

FREQUENTLY ASKED QUESTIONS

At the beginning of each of our seminars, we tell our participants, "While we are talking, we would like for you to be thinking of questions you want to ask us. *Feel free to ask us anything at all, because you will be asking the questions anonymously.* We ask that you write down your questions, and we'll pass a hat around to collect the written questions. At the end of the seminar, we'll answer the questions for the benefit of everyone—and no one will know who asked what!"

We've found that some of the same questions are asked over and over again. Some of the most frequently asked questions are addressed here.

How does one know for sure that getting a divorce is the right thing to do? It is a scary step and I am not sure I would be doing what is right.

One of our seminar participants shared with the others that she had thought long and hard before she decided to get a divorce. She said that she and her husband had tried self-help books, seminars, and marriage counseling for several years, and that finally she was able to take action after reading an article in a magazine that suggested that people in this situation use the acronym "ACT."

Accept that the situation is not going to change. If you have tried everything within your power—such as professional counseling, seminars, and self-help books—and nothing has worked, accept it. You are not going to change him. You can only change yourself and your situation.

Choose what you *do* want from life. Read chapter 2, "Divorced," to learn what you will experience during your divorce. Are you ready for that commitment? If so, then set your priorities. You may have to give up some of the material aspects of your present life. Be very sure that you are willing to do this. You will know that *you* have chosen to relinquish those things in favor of your new life. Set your goals and imagine yourself in that new life. (See chapter 6, "Your Personal Bank Account of Life Experiences," chapter 7, "Setting and Accomplishing Your Goals," and chapter 8, "Landing a Job or Starting a Business.")

Take action if you have realistically weighted the pros and cons, and divorce is your solution.

I have been widowed for over four months now, and there are still times when my grief overwhelms me. Do you have any tips for me?

Give yourself a year's time. That's a year to feel shock, anger, depression, acceptance. That's a year when you try to avoid making big, earth-shaking decisions.

During that year try all the tips and ideas in this book, lean on your friends, and follow the dictates of your heart.

Give yourself a year's time, but know that grief has its own timetable, and will not be rushed or slowed by our whims or desires. If necessary, give yourself longer. If you still feel overwhelmed, call your local hospice for names of support groups. Don't hesitate to seek professional help.

How does one start to gain self-confidence?
- Make yourself as attractive to yourself as you can. Wear your favorite bright colors.
- The more secure and in control you feel about your financial situation, the more self-confident and self-sufficient you will become. Educate yourself about all facets of your finances—salary, retirement benefits, investments, and all insurance—life, health, home, auto. (See chapter 10, "Protecting Your Assets"; chapter 11, "Buying or Selling a Home"; chapter 12, "New Car Fever"; and chapter 13, "Traveling.")

SURVIVAL TIP

Several inspiring books about women who have "made it on their own" are: *Personal History,* by Katharine Graham (Alfred Knopf, 1996); *Bouncing Back,* by Joan Rivers (HarperCollins, 1997); *The Other Side of the Mountain,* by E. G. Valens (HarperCollins, 1989); and *The Uncommon Wisdom of Oprah Winfrey,* edited by Bill Adler (William Morrow, 1996).

- Be realistic in your goal setting. If you need computer skills to land the job you want, give yourself time to complete the required computer courses. If you need to take off some weight, set a realistic time period. Have patience with yourself in attaining your goals. (See chapter 7, "Setting and Accomplishing Your Goals.")
- Call your local United Way or mental health association for referral to organizations that offer seminars on self-confidence. Attend at least three seminars.
- Check the curriculum offered by the continuing-education department of your local college for courses on self-confidence. Enroll and attend faithfully.
- Is there a Dale Carnegie course on self-confidence offered in your area? Find out and enroll in one.

- Talk to yourself. Keep telling yourself, "I *know* I can. I *know* I can.
- Pat yourself on the back. Every small step forward is a triumph. Have you just finished updating your resumé? Congratulate yourself! Have you established your own line of credit with a bank? Hooray for you!

I really miss being included with my "old group" of married friends. I am included for lunch with the women, but I am excluded from dinner and theater parties with the husbands. What can I do?

See chapter 14, "Socializing and Dating Again."

My children are newly married. How can I help them so that they will not end up with the same uncommunicative relationship that their father and I had?

Be honest. Explain to them that you are aware that your relationship with their father was not a communicative one.

Encourage them to stay sensitive to any facet of their relationship where communication may be faltering.

Encourage them to face the problem if they confide that there is one. It's so easy for relationships to fall into bad communication habits, just because one or the other doesn't have the energy or courage to talk about a problem when it begins to occur.

Advise them to seek professional help together if they cannot solve the problem themselves. Again, the earlier the better.

How can I get my fiancé to divulge financial information and discuss future budgeting? In the two years that I have dated him, I have come to know a loving, giving, and generous person, but I have been unsuccessful in getting him to talk about money and our future financial security. Naturally it is causing no small amount of resentment in me.

See chapter 14, "Socializing and Dating Again."

SUCCESS STORIES

Nothing is more rewarding to us than to hear from our seminar participants about their walks onward and upward. Here are some excerpts from their letters:

"I am feeling and doing much better. I have carved out a schedule for myself which has structure to it, and which keeps me busy several evenings a week. I am taking a class at the college— my classmates don't know what to do with me—I'm as new an experience for them as they are for me!—CAC

"Those wonderful promises you made about life getting better now have truth for me."—RSB

"I'm finally looking forward to getting up in the morning. I have planned a nice trip and am concentrating on getting my son into college. Then I'm going to use some of my skills from my volunteer work to get a part-time job."—SM

"Early on, I found a financial adviser I really trust and respect, but now prefer to make most of the choices on my own. And the portfolio was up 16 percent last year!—MBA

"I have accepted dinner invitations with a couple of male friends—and that's what we are just now—friends. I'm cautiously wondering about romance and what it would be like at my age. Things are looking up, and one of the greatest helps I've had is your assurance that it would get better, and that you cared."—RBC

You are now ready to go onward and upward with your life. As the years pass, you will look back on this time in your life as a momentary "bump in the road." There have been times when we have said to each other, "You know, it wasn't so bad." Then we remember that yes, it *was* so bad. We have just forgotten. The terror we felt for our futures has dimmed with the passing of time, as it will for you. Adversity is a part of life. Without adversity in our own lives, we cannot hope to gain empathy for the sufferings of others.

How one responds to adversity is what is important. If we try to blame someone else for our adversity, then we will not grow.

We all have choices in life. Choose to face your adversity, conquer it, learn from it, use it, and move on. If we had not experienced these monumental transitions in our lives, we never would have had our dream career, we would never have had an opportunity to help and comfort others with our seminars, and, certainly, we would never have written a book.

We encourage you to continue to grow through all your life's experiences and go *onward and upward*. When adversity comes, remember, "God never gives us more than we can handle!"

BIBLIOGRAPHY

BUSINESS

AARP. *Divorce After 50: Challenges and Choices.* Washington, D.C.: AARP, 1987.

Barker, Becky. *Answers.* New York: Harper & Row, 1984.

Boardroom Books. *The Book of Inside Information, Bottom Line Personal, A Collection of the Advice of Expert Authorities.* New York: Boardroom Classics, 1987.

Briles, Judith. *The Dollars and Sense of Divorce.* New York: Ballantine Books, 1988.

Burczeller, Dr. Peter H. "How to Deal With Your Doctor More Effectively," *Bottom Line Personal,* June 15, 1994.

Charell, Ralph. *Satisfaction Guaranteed.* Stillwater, Minn.: Linden Press, 1985.

Godfrey, Joline. *Our Wildest Dreams.* New York: Harper Business, 1992.

Huff, Priscilla Y. *101 Best Small Businesses for Women.* Rocklyn, Calif.: Prima Publishing, 1996.

Martin, Don and Renee Martin. *The Survival Guide for Women.* Washington, D.C.: Regnery Gateway, 1991.

Wall, Ginita and the editors of Consumer Reports Books. *Our Money, Our Selves: Money Management for Each Stage of a Woman's Life.* Yonkers, N.Y.: Consumer Reports Books, 1992.

Wesman, Jane. *Dive Right In—The Sharks Won't Bite.* Paramus, N.J.: Prentice Hall Division of Simon and Schuster, 1995.

White, Shelby. *What Every Woman Should Know About Her Husband's Money.* New York: Random House, 1992.

Whittelsey, Frances Cerra. *Why Women Pay More: How to Avoid Marketplace Perils,* Washington, D.C.: Center for Study for Responsive Law, 1993.

Zuckerman, Laurie B. *On Your Own.* Dover, N.H.: Upstart Publishing, 1993.

CAREERS

Bolles, Richard Nelson. *What Color Is Your Parachute?* Berkeley, Calif.: Ten Speed Press, 1995.

LOSS AND GRIEF

Alderman, Linda. *Why Did Daddy Die? Helping Children Cope With the Loss of A Parent.* New York: Pocket Books, 1991.

Brooks, Anne M. *The Grieving Time: A Year's Account of Recovery From Loss.* New York: Doubleday & Co., 1988.

Buscaglia, Leo. *The Fall of Freddie the Leaf: A Story of Life for All Ages.* New York: Henry Holt, 1982.

Cherry, Frank, and John W. James. *The Grief Recovery Handbook, A Step-by-Step Program for Moving Beyond Loss.* New York: Harper Perennial, 1988.

Colgrove, Melba, Ph.D., Harold Bloomfield, M.D., and Peter McWilliams. *How to Survive the Loss of a Love.* New York: Bantam Books, 1976.

Gravelle, Karen, and Charles Haskins. *Teenagers Face to Face With Bereavement.* Parsippany, N.J.: Silver Burdett Press, 1989.

LeShan, Eda. *Learning to Say Good-bye: When A Parent Dies.* Old Tappan, N.J.: Simon & Schuster, 1976.

Stein, Sara Bonnett. *About Dying: An Open Family Book for Parents and Children Together.* New York: Walker, 1974.

Westberg, Granger E. *Good Grief.* Philadelphia Penn.: Fortress Press, 1971.

MOTIVATION

Adler, Bill. *The Uncommon Wisdom of Oprah Winfrey.* New York: William Morrow, 1996.

Graham, Katharine. *Personal History.* New York: Alfred Knopf, 1996.

Hansen, Mark Victor. *Future Diary.* Newport Beach, Calif.: Mark Victor Hansen, 1983.

Jeffers, Susan, Ph.D. *Feel the Fear and Do It Anyway.* New York: Fawcett Columbine, 1987.

Hunter, Frances. *Hotline to Heaven.* Kingwood, Tex.: Hunter Books, 1970.

Myers, David G., Ph.D. *The Pursuit of Happiness.* New York: Avon Books, 1992.

Rivers, Joan. *Bouncing Back.* New York: HarperCollins, 1997.

Robertson, John and Betty Utterback. *Suddenly Single: Learning to Start Over Through the Experience of Others.* New York: Simon and Schuster, 1986.

Schlessinger, Laura, Ph.D. *Ten Stupid Things Women Do to Mess Up Their Lives.* New York, Harper Perennial, 1995.

Two Listeners. *God Calling.* New York: Dodd, Mead & Co., 1945.

Valens, E.G. *The Other Side of the Mountain.* New York: HarperCollins, 1989.

Williams, Leslie. *Night Wrestling.* Dallas, Tex.: Word Publishing, 1997.

INDEX

AAA. *See* American Automobile
    Association
AARP. *See* American Association of
    Retired Persons
Acceptance as stage of grief, 18–19,
    55–57, 59
Accidental death, 45
Accion Internacional, 122
Accountants, 129–30, 146
Action plan in goal planning, 104
Addictions, 206
Adjustable rate mortgages (ARMs), 174
Age, 88, 103, 111
Alarm clocks, 8
Alarm systems, 5
Aldridge, Roberta, 167
Alimony, 34, 36–37
Aloneness, 3–11
    at night, 4–7
    during the day, 8–11
    in the morning, 7–8
Alpers, John H., 131, 134, 142–43, 144
Alternate plan in goal planning, 104–5,
    107
Alzheimer's disease, 155
American Association of Retired
    Persons (AARP), 129
American Automobile Association
    (AAA), 190
American Homeowners Association,
    216
American Society of Home Inspectors,
    171
Amtrak, 193
Anger, 10
    at husband, 16
    at self, 16
    as stage of grief, 15–17, 50, 52–53
Annuities, 145–46
Antiques, 144

Appetite, 9, 50
Appliances, 170
Appointment calendars, 8
ARMs. *See* Adjustable rate mortgages
Assertiveness, 76–84
Assets, 213–15
    annuities, 145–46
    list of, 215
    money, 137–42
    in probate, 44, 48, 49
    real, 144
    See also Investments
AT&T's directory of toll-free numbers,
    80
Attorneys. *See* Lawyers
Auto auctions, 185
Auto Safety Hotline, 186
Automobile Clubs, 190
Automobiles. *See* Cars

Baby Boomers, xi
Baggage on planes, 192
Bank accounts, 43
    for estates, 48
Bankruptcy, 126
Bar association, 127
Bargaining in buying cars, 180, 186, 212
Basic daily activities, 155
Benefits, spousal, 215–16
Berczeller, Peter H., "How to Deal With
    Your Doctor More Effectively,"
    81–82
Best's Insurance Reports, 134, 145
Better Business Bureau, 132, 181
Bills, paying, 214
Bitterness, 17
Blind dates, 203
Blue-chip stocks, 143
Bonds, 48, 143
Bookkeeping, 139

Bottom Line Personal (magazine), 81
Burglaries, 43
Business
    funding for, 120–22
    plans for, 120
    starting your own, 99, 118–22, 125,
        223
Business and Professional Women's
    Foundation, xi
Buying a car, 178–86, 212
Buying a home, 126, 169–77
Buying versus renting, 176–77

Capital gains taxes, 163
Captive agents, 133
Car and Driver (magazine), 178
Careers, xi–xii
    discovering, 85–99
    new, 10, 60
    See also Jobs
Cars
    auto auctions, 185
    Auto Safety Hotline, 186
    automobile clubs, 190
    brokers for buying, 180–81
    buying new, 178–81, 212
    buying used, 184–86, 212
    insurance for, 157–59, 179, 213
    leasing, 182–84
    loans for buying, 182
    maintenance of, 212
    recalls on, 186
    rental expense insurance for, 158
    rentals of, 193
    selling by owners, 181–82
Cash on hand, 215
Cash value funds, 149
Cellular phones, 190
Certified Financial Planner (CFP), 132
Certified Life Underwriter (CLU), 135
Certified Public Accountant (CPA), 129
CFP. *See* Certified Financial Planner
Chambers of commerce, 101, 121
Charell, Ralph, *Satisfaction Guaranteed*,
    80
Chartered Financial Consultant (ChFC),
    132
Chartered Property and Casualty
    Underwriter (CPCU), 135
Check register/ledger, 45, 138
Checking accounts, 137–39, 213
ChFC. *See* Chartered Financial
    Consultant
Children
    custody of, 34–36

day care for, 101
grief of, 57–59
guardians for, 217
marriages of, 220
support for, 34, 35–36
Choices, making, 77, 221
Churches, 101, 200
Clergy, 57
CLU. *See* Certified Life Underwriter
COBRA act, 152, 213
Coffee. *See* Stimulants
Collateral, 27, 121, 122
College, 36, 100–102
    courses for self-confidence, 219
    for job/career, 109
College placement offices, 111
Commingling of property, 47
*Commissioners Standard Ordinary
    Mortality and Disabilities Tables*,
    153
Commissions
    for financial planners, 133, 146
    for insurance agents, 136
Community property states, 31
Complaining about products or
    services, 79–80
Computer literacy, 99, 101, 139, 219
Computers, bookkeeping software for,
    139
Concern for Dying, 161
Condominiums, 171
Confusion, 10
Consumer Credit Counseling, 215
Consumer Information Center, 80
Consumer protection, 79–80
Consumer Reports, 178, 179, 212
Consumer Reports Used Car Price
    Service, 185, 212
Consumer's Guide, 79
Consumer's Resource Handbook, 80
Contingency fees for lawyers, 128
Cooperatives, 171
Cost of living, 110
Counseling
    for grief, 57
    seeking, 10–11, 101, 219
County health department, 11, 57
Court orders, 13
Cover letters, 114–16
CPAs. *See* Certified public accountants
CPCU. *See* Chartered Property and
    Casualty Underwriter
Credit cards, 26, 45, 141–42, 191, 196,
    214
Credit history, 28, 139, 141, 142

Credit rating, 139–42, 214
Credit Reporting Agencies, 142
Crying, 4, 53
Custody of children, 34–36

Dale Carnegie courses, 219
Dating, 200–210
  blind, 203
  general rules for, 204–6
  getting serious, 206–7
  meeting men, 202–3
  obstacles to, 201–2
  prenuptual agreements, 207–10
  right and wrong reasons for, 200–201
Dead-bolt locks, 5
Dealer costs of new cars, 179
Death certificates, 41
Death tax returns, 47
Debt instruments, 143–44
Debts
  personal, 214, 215
  in probate, 44, 49
Decisions, major. See Major decisions
Deductible
  in car insurance, 213
  in health insurance, 151
Deferred annuities, 145
Degrees. See College
Denial as stage of grief, 50–52
Dependent coverage in health
    insurance, 151
Depreciated cost homeowner's
    insurance, 155
Depression, 10
  as stage of grief, 17–18, 52–53
Diarrhea, 9, 50
Dinner parties, 199
Directory of Community Services, 101
Disability insurance, 152–54
Disclosure requirements, 166
Discount travel services, 195
Dividend and interest income, 48, 143,
    148–49
Division of assets in divorce, 24, 29–34
Divorce, 12–39, 217–18
  and children, 14, 34–36
  division of assets in, 24, 29–34
  finalization of, 24, 37–38
  lawyers for, 13, 19–24, 126–27
  making the decision, 12–13
  mediators for, 23, 38
  no-fault, 25
  planning for, 12–14
  separation in, 13–14, 24–29
  and social security, 37

and state laws, 31, 38
  statistics on, xi
  temporary support in, 25–26, 28–29
Divorce and Annulments, U.S. Bureau
    of the Census, xi
Doctors. See Medical professionals
Down payments, 169, 172, 175, 177
Drive-up appeal, 165
Drugs for sleep, 6
Duff & Phelps, 135
Durable power of attorney, 161
Durable power of attorney for health
    care, 161

Earthquakes, 155
Eating properly. See Food
Electrical circuits, 170
Employee Retirement Income
    Securities Act, 33
Employment agencies, 111
Employment service, 110, 111
Encore (travel club), 195
Enrolled agents, 130
Equities, 143
Equity in homes, 176–77
ERISA. See Employee Retirement
    Income Securities Act
Escrow payments, 174
Estate attorneys, 146
Estate planning, 132, 147
Evaluation of outcome in goal
    planning, 105, 107
Exclusions
  in health insurance, 151
  in homeowner's insurance, 155–56
Execution of plan in goal planning, 105,
    107
Executor of estate, 43, 44, 126, 217
  choosing, 160
  duties of, 46–49
  working with, 45
Exercising, 10, 80, 212
Experiences, life, 85–99

Factory rebates, 179
Family, financial status of, xi, 13, 30
Family allowance, 45
Family Services, 57
Fantasizing, 105
Fears, listing of, 4
Federal Housing Administration
    (FHA), 174, 175, 176
Fee-and-commission financial
    planners, 146
Feelings, writing about, 6, 52

FHA. *See* Federal Housing
    Administration
Finalization of divorce, 24, 37–38
Finances, 60
    business, 120–22
    discussion of, 108–10, 220
    of family, xi, 13, 30
    income needs, 110
    temporary support worksheet, 28–29
    See also Credit cards; Credit history;
        Credit rating; Line of credit
Financial aid for college, 100, 101
Financial plan, 131–32
Financial planners, 130–34, 144, 146
    choosing, 132–34
    in death of husband, 44
    fees for, 133, 146
    reasons for hiring, 131–32
Financial statements, 30, 120
"Finding a Job or Starting Your Own
    Business" workshop, 118
First impressions, 165–66
Fixed deferred annuities, 145
Fixed rate mortgages, 173–74
Flat fees
    for financial planners, 133, 146
    for insurance agents, 136
    for lawyers, 24, 127
    for tax preparation, 130
Floods, 155
Flowers and memorials, 42
Food
    for breakfast, 8
    eating nutritious, 9, 80
Foreign traveling, 194–97
Formal wills, 159
Friends
    calling, 7, 9, 83
    in death of husband, 40, 42–43
    fear of imposing on, 55
    going out with, 199
    making new, 9, 200
    married, 220
    offers of help from, 9, 15
    and support groups, 63–66
Funeral arrangements, 41–43

Gap insurance, 184
Gas, 144
Gateway Financial Strategies, 131, 134,
    142–43
Gift taxes, 147
Goals
    for future, 131
    setting and accomplishing, 100–107
Grandma Moses, 103
Graveside services, 42
Grief
    of children, 57–59
    getting help for, 57–58
    stages of, 14–19
    in widowhood, 50–57, 318–19
Grooming in the morning, 8
Growth-enhancing transitions, xii
Guaranteed-income account, 145
Guardian for children, 217
Guilt and grief, 53–54
Gynecology examinations, 212

Hansen, Mark Victor, 106
Happiness, permission for, 11, 56
Hayes, Christopher, xii
Health, 212
Health insurance, 151–52, 213
Health Insurance Association of
    America, *What You Should Know
    About Health Insurance*, 152
Holographic wills, 159
Home health care, 154, 155
Home inspections, 164, 171
Homeowner's insurance, 155–57
*Homeowners Property Tax Reduction
    Kit, The*, 216
Homes
    as assets, 144
    best time to buy, 170
    buying, 126, 169–77
    care and maintenance of, 213
    in divorce, 34
    equity in, 176–77
    fixing up tips, 166–68
    loans for buying, 172–76
    offers to buy, 171
    renting versus buying, 176–77
    resale value of, 170
    security check of, 5
    selling, 126, 162–69
    selling by owners, 168–69
    showings for selling, 168
Hospice counselors, 51, 57
Hospices, 41, 59, 101, 219
Hospital preadmission authorization,
    152
Hotels, 194
Hourly fees
    for lawyers, 23, 45, 127
    for tax preparation, 130
Household inventory records, 156

Housing assistance, 101
"How to Deal With Your Doctor More
    Effectively" (Berczeller), 81–82

Immune systems, 9
Income needs, 110
Income tax returns, 30, 31, 48
Inflation-protection clauses, 156
Inheritances, 32
Inheritors, 46, 47
Injunctions, 13
Inner peace, 19
Institute of Certified Financial
    Planners Consumer Assistance
    Line, 132
Insulation, 170
Insurance, 31, 213
    car, 157–59, 179, 213
    casualty, 134
    credit card, 45
    disability, 134, 152–54
    double coverage, 135
    gap, 184
    health, 135, 151–52, 213
    homeowner's, 155–57
    life, 134, 147–51, 213
    long-term care, 154–55
    mortgage, 169, 174–76
    personal property, 155–56
    warranty, 165
Insurance agents, 134–36, 136, 146
Insurance industry, 43–44, 134
Insurance Institute for Highway Safety,
    179
Intellichoice, 179
Interest on debts, 214
Interest on mortgages, 172, 173, 176
Interest rates, 150, 173
Interest-bearing checking accounts, 138
Internal Revenue Code, 216
Internal Revenue Service, 31, 125, 129,
    130
International Association for Financial
    Planning, 132
Internet
    job postings on, 111
    Medi-Net, 212
    meeting men on, 203
    surfing, 81
Interviews for jobs, 116–18
Intestate, 49
Intuition, 207
Investment products, 133
Investments, 78, 142–46
    categories of, 143–44

in financial plan, 132
IRAs, 31
Irrevocable living trusts, 160–61
IRS. See Internal Revenue Service
Isolation feelings in grief, 50–51

Jewelry, 144
Job Training Partnership, 101
Jobs
    considering an offer, 118
    cover letters, 114–16
    discrimination in, 127
    finding, 108–18
    interviews for, 116–18
    networking for, 110–11
    resumé writing, 111–14
    skills and needs assesment, 109–10
    See also Careers
"Jobs and Careers" workshop, 108
Joint legal child custody, 35
Joint tenancy, 159
Journal keeping, 6
Junior League, 101

Kells, Ruth, 103
Keogh funds, 31

Langston Realtors, 167
Lawyers
    choosing, 19–21, 127–28
    for divorce, 13, 19–24, 126–27
    fees for, 23–24, 44–45, 127–28
    free services of, 128
    need for, 125–27
    probating wills, 44
    working with, 21–23, 30
Leasing cars, 182–84
Leasing with option to buy, 177
Legal name, 26–27, 140, 214
Legal Services Corporation, 128
Legatees, 46, 47
"Lemon laws," 184
Letters testamentary, 44, 48
Liability insurance, 156–57
Life experiences, 85–99
Life insurance, 147–51
    and estate planning, 147, 160
    need for, 213
    proceeds in death, 44, 48, 149, 159
"Life Strategies" seminars, 53, 200, 211
Line of credit, 27–28, 140, 214
Lists
    for anger, 15–16
    at work, 84
    for depression, 17

Lists (*cont'd.*)
  of fears, 4
  for support groups, 65–66
  of things to do, 9, 15
  of worries, 6
Living trusts, 44, 60, 160–61
Living wills, 161
Loans
  for business, 120–22
  for buying cars, 182
  for buying homes, 172–76
  for establishing line of credit, 27
  rated, 140
Locks, dead-bolt, 5
Long Island University, xii
Long-term care insurance, 154–55
"Lunch Bunch," 63–64

Maiden name, 26–27, 214
Major decisions, 10, 163, 218
Major medical policies, 151
"Managing Your Money," 139
Medi-Net, 212
Mediators for divorce, 23, 38
Medicaid, 154
Medical professionals, 80–82, 212
Medicare, 155
Meditation, 10
Meir, Golda, 103
Memorial services, 42
Mental health organizations, 101, 219
Mercer, Mark, 51
Minorities in small businesses, 122
Money, 137–42, 196–97, 213–15
Money magazine, 79, 145
Money market checking accounts,
  138–39
Monthly living expenses, 45
Moody's, 134
Morningstar ratings, 145–46
Mortgage insurance, 169, 174–76
Mortgage payments, 163
Mortgages, 172–76, 215
Motion sensor lights, 5
Motor Trend (magazine), 179
Mourning process. *See* Stages of grief
Mud slides, 155
Multiple-listing services, 164
Music, 10
Mutual funds, 48, 139, 143, 145
Mystical experiences, 51

Names, legal and maiden, 26–27, 140, 214
*National Automobile Dealers
  Association Official Used-Car*

Guide, 186
National Center for Health Statistics, xi
National Center for Women and
  Retirement Research, xii
National Insurance Consumer Hotline,
  158
National Taxpayers Union, 216
National Underwirter Company, *Who
  Writes What in Life and Health
  Insurance*, 152
Nausea, 9, 50
Negative thoughts, 6, 8, 10
Negotiating in buying cars, 180, 186,
  212
Networking
  for jobs, 110
  and small businesses, 121
Newspaper classified sections, 111
Night aloneness, 4–7
No-fault divorces, 25, 31
Non-custodial parent, 35
Nursing homes, 154

Obituaries, 41, 42, 43
Objectives in goal planning, 103–4, 107
Oil, 144
Opportunities in problems, 10
Organ donors, 41
Overpricing of homes, 165

Pain, patience with, 14
Pallbearers, 42
Partnerships, 49
Passports, 195–96
Paying bills, 214
Peace, inner, 19
Penny stocks, 143
Pension plans, 31, 32–33, 48, 144, 147
  spousal share of, 215–16
  See also Retirement
Percentage fees for lawyers, 127–28
Permanent child custody, 35
Personal injury settlements, 32
Personal property insurance, 155–56
Phone calling cards, 197
Phones, cellular, 190
Pity parties, 17
Plane travel, 191–92
Plans
  for accomplishing goals, 103–7
  for the day, 8
  for emergencies, 5
  long-range, 59–60
  worksheet for goal planning, 106–7
Points, 173

Positive thinking, 8
Poverty levels, xi, 154
Powers of attorney, 60, 132, 161
Preexisting conditions, 151, 152
Prenuptial ageements, 127, 207–10
Prepayment penalties, 174
Presurgery review, 152
Price discrimination, 79–80
Privacy, 18
Probate process, 44, 45, 48, 126, 159
Problems as opportunities, 10
Professional degrees, 36
Professionals, 123–36
    financial planners, 130–34
    general rules for choosing, 124–25
    insurance agents, 134–36
    lawyers, 125–28
    See also Counseling
Profit sharing, 48
Proofreading, 114
Property commingling, 47
Property taxes, 163, 176, 216
Public-speaking courses, 99

Qualified domestic relations order
    (QDRO), 216
Qualified Terminal Interest Property
    (QTIP) election, 49
Questions asked frequently, 217–20
"Quicken," 139
Quiz and short review, 212–17

Range fees, for lawyers, 24, 127
Real assets, 144
Real estate, 144
Realtors
    choosing, 164–65
    commissions of, 163
Rebate travel agencies, 194–95
Recalls on cars, 186
References, 114
Referrals
    for jobs, 110–11
    for lawyers, 20
Registered Investment Adviser (RIA),
    131, 133, 134
Regular checking accounts, 138
Relatives, 40
Relief and grief, 54
Rental car agencies, 185, 193
Rental property, 144
Renter's insurance, 156
Renting versus buying, 176–77
Replacement cost homeowner's
    insurance, 155

Resource allocation in goal planning,
    104, 107
Resources
    for career planning, 224
    for children's grief, 59
    for loss and grief, 224
    for motivation, 224–25
    for self-confidence, 219–20
    for starting businesses, 99, 223
Restraining orders, 13
Resumé writing, 111–14
Retainers for lawyers, 23–24, 127
Retirement
    in financial plan, 132
    needs for, 131
    planning for, 31, 45, 144, 147, 159, 215
    See also Pensions
Revocable living trusts, 160–61
RIA. See Registered Investment Adviser
Risk protection in financial plan, 131
Risk tolerance, 131, 143, 146
Robbins, Tony, 105
Routine, breaking out of, 10

S corportations, 49
Sadness, 10
Safe-deposit boxes, 156, 217
Sanity, questioning about, 51
Satisfaction Guaranteed (Charell), 80
Savings, 131, 215
SBA. See Small Business
    Administration
Scholarships, 101
Sears Discount Travel Club, 195
SEC. See Securities and Exchange
    Commission
Second opinions, 81
Second-to-die life insurance, 149
Securities and Exchange Commission
    (SEC), 133
Self-confidence, 219–20
Self-doubt, 86–87
Self-fulfilling prophecy, 105
Selling a home, 126, 162–69
Seminars, xiii
    on "Life Strategies," 53, 200, 211
    on loss, 14
    success stories from, 220–21
    See also Workshops
Senior citizens' discounts, 191, 192, 194,
    195
Separation in divorce, 13–14, 24–29
Settlement agreemeent, 38
Shock, 4
    as stage of grief, 14–15, 50–52

Shock (cont'd.)
  symptoms of, 9, 50
Signed settlement agreement, 38
Skills, new, 10
Skills worksheets, 90–99
Sleep
  alcohol or drugs for, 6, 7
  problems with, 50
  when to, 7
Small Business Administration (SBA),
    121
Small Business Development Centers,
    121
Smart Money (magazine), 145
Smart Traveler, The, 195
Social Security
  benefits from, 45, 48
  and divorce, 37
  of husband, 216
  and retirement, 147
Social Security Administration, 216
Social Security disability, 126, 153
Social service organizations, 101
Socializing and dating, 199–210
Sole child custody, 35
Solid-core doors, 5
Spiritual beliefs, 8, 206
Spousal benefits, 215–16
Spousal support. See Alimony
Stages of grief, 14–19
  in widowhood, 50–57
Standard & Poor's, 134
Standard of living and financial plan,
    131
Statistics, xi
Statutory wills, 159
Stimulants, 6–7, 8, 84
Stock redemption, 49
Stockbrokers, 48, 146
Stocks, 48, 49, 143, 144
Strange experiences, 51
Stucker, Jan Collins, xi
Success stories, 220–21
Summary of Veterans Administration
    Benefits, Veterans Administration,
    45
Support
  alimony, 36–37
  child, 34, 35–36
  temporary, 25–26, 28–29
Support groups, 57, 59, 63–75, 101, 219
  format of, 73–74
  joining existing group, 75
  list of people for, 65–66
  roles played in, 71–72

rules for, 69–71, 72–73
size of, 66
where and when to meet, 67–69
Survival techniques, x

Tax attorneys, 146
Tax preparers, 129–30
  availablity of, 216–17
  in divorce, 31
Tax-Aide Centers, 129
Taxes, 46, 47, 216–17
  and annuities, 145
  deferred, 144, 149
  and divorce, 34
  estate, 44, 49, 132, 147, 160
  gift, 147
  and interest, 176
  property, 163, 176, 216
Temporary child custody, 35
Temporary support, 25–26
Temporary support worksheet, 28–29
Term life insurance, 148
Termites, 170, 171
Testamentary trusts, 160
Time, 102–3
Title searches, 171
Toll-free numbers directory, 80
Towing insurance, 158–59
Town houses, 171
Train travel, 192–93
Transitions, x, xii
Travel agents, 190–91
Travel Avenue, 195
Traveler's checks, 196
Traveling, 189–98
  by plane, 191–92
  by train, 192–93
  discount travel services, 195
  foreign, 195–97
  hotels, 194
  money-saving vacations, 194–95
  preparing for, 198
  rebate travel agencies, 194–95
  travel clubs, 195
Trusts, 60, 159, 160–61

Umbrella policies, 156–57
United Way, 57, 101, 219
Universal life insurance, 150
U.S. Bureau of the Census, Divorce and
    Annulments, xi
Used car dealers, 79
Utility costs, 166, 170

Vacations, 194–95

See also Traveling
Variable deferred annuities, 145
Variable life insurance, 150–51
Veterans Administration, *Summary of
    Veterans Administration Benefits*,
    45, 48
VITA. *See* Volunteer Income Tax
    Assistance
Vitamins, 80
Vocational skills, 101
Volunteer Income Tax Assistance
    (VITA) program, 129
Volunteer skills, 38, 111
Volunteering, 200

Warner, Jan L., xi
Warranty insurance, 165
Wedding rings, 56–57
Weiss Research, Inc., 135
*What You Should Know About Health
    Insurance*, Health Insurance
    Association of America, 152
Whittelsey, Frances Cerra, *Why Women
    Pay More: How to Avoid
    Marketplace Perils*, 79
*Who Writes What in Life and Health
    Insurance*, National Underwriter
    Company, 152
Whole life insurance, 148–51
*Why Women Pay More: How to Avoid
    Marketplace Perils* (Whittelsey), 79
Widowhood, 40–60, 218–19
    checklist for, 43–45
    funeral arrangements, 41–43
    notifying others of death, 42–43

settling the estate, 43–49
statistics on, xi
viewing the body, 40
Wills, 46, 125–26, 159–61, 217
    and estate planning, 147
    intestate, 49
    living, 161
    probate process for, 44
    revising, 45, 60
    types of, 159
Window guards, 5
Women
    as consumers, 79–80
    discounts on auto insurance for, 158
    and medical professionals, 80–82
    in small businesses, 121, 122
    statistics on, xi
"Women in Transition" workshop, xi, 17
Workmen's compensation, 126
Workplace, xi
    during grief, 83–84
    reentering, 101, 108–18
Worksheets
    for goal planning, 106–7
    for skills assesment, 90–99
Workshops, xi, xiii
    "Finding a Job or Starting Your Own
        Business, 118
    "Jobs and Careers," 108
    See also Seminars
Worries, list of, 6

Ziglar, Zig, 8
Zoning, 169